PHOTOGRAPHY
OUTDOORS

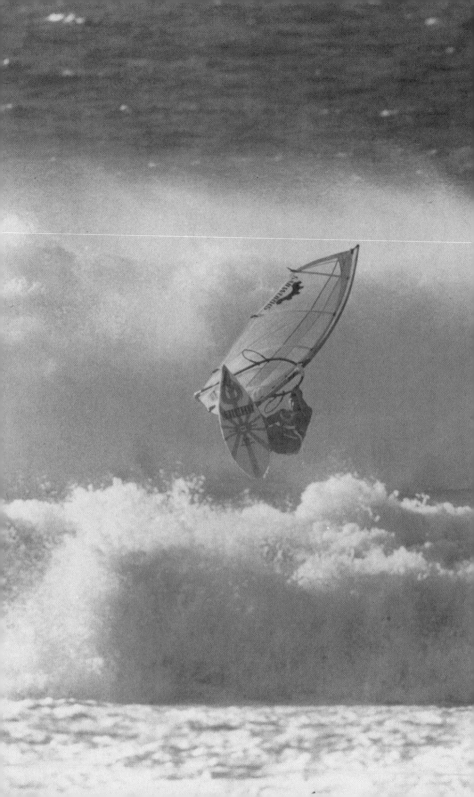

PHOTOGRAPHY

A FIELD GUIDE FOR TRAVEL
& ADVENTURE PHOTOGRAPHERS

OUTDOORS

MARK GARDNER
& ART WOLFE

THE
MOUNTAINEERS

Published by
The Mountaineers
1001 SW Klickitat Way, Suite 201
Seattle, Washington 98134

© 1995 by Mark Gardner and Art Wolfe
Color photographs © Art Wolfe
Figures 1-1–1-5, 2-1, 2-2, 3-1–3-3, 5-2, 5-5, 5-7, 5-11, 5-12, and pp. 8 and 11
© Art Wolfe
Figures 4-1–4-5, 5-1, 5-6, 5-8–5-10 © Mark Gardner
Figures 5-3, 5-4 © Carl Skoog

First edition: first printing 1995, second printing 1995, third printing 1997,
fourth printing 1998

Published simultaneously in Great Britain by Cordee, 3a DeMontfort Street,
Leicester, England, LE1 7HD

Manufactured in the United States of America

Edited by Kris Fulsaas
All photographs by Art Wolfe unless otherwise noted
Cover design by Elizabeth Watson
Book design, layout and typography by The Mountaineers Books

Cover photograph: Silhouette/Photographer at Sunset, Washington Coast,
© Art Wolfe
Frontispiece: Windsurfers, Maui, Hawaii © Art Wolfe

Library of Congress Cataloging-in-Publication Data
Gardner, Mark, 1953–
    Photography outdoors : a field guide for travel and adventure
photographers / Mark Gardner and Art Wolfe.
        p.   cm.
    Includes bibliographical references (p.   ) and index.
    ISBN 0-89886-430-5
    1. Outdoor photography.   I. Wolfe, Art.   II. Title.
    TR659.5.G37   1995
    778.7'1—dc20   95–17487
                                                                CIP

♻ Printed on recycled paper

CONTENTS

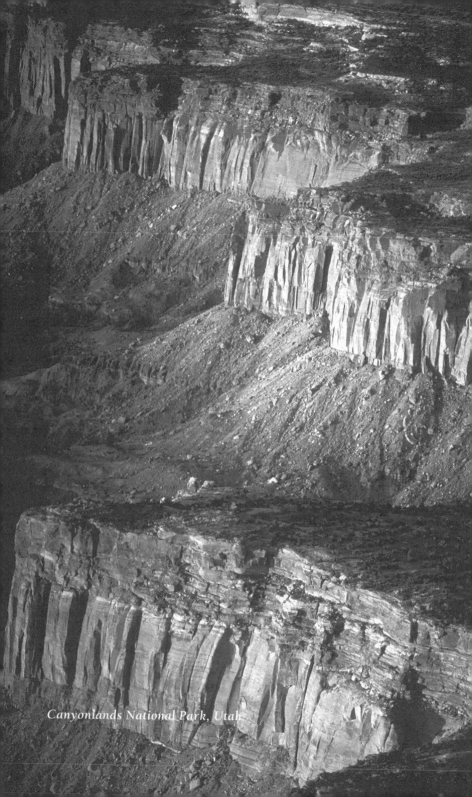

Canyonlands National Park, Utah

INTRODUCTION

ADVENTURE PHOTOGRAPHY

For the most part, adventure photography is just like any other type of photography applied to the scenes and activities enjoyed while on adventures. However, there are several important differences. First, you often have limited camera equipment. On most adventures, the amount of gear you can take is limited to what you can carry on your back or fit into one or two travel bags along with all the rest of your gear. Thus you usually do not have the luxury of carrying a full complement of lenses and accessories. In fact, sometimes you may be limited to a camera with a single lens, maybe an extra lens, a handful of film, and a few key accessories. So you should choose your gear wisely and learn to get the most out of what you do take.

Second, you often have limited time. Great photography usually requires plenty of time to work the scene to get the best possible image. But adventures are often too short and move too quickly to provide the luxury of taking lots of time for photography. So you have to allow extra time for shooting and take full advantage of what time you do have by thorough preparation. Before actually taking any pictures, spend time thinking through what you want to shoot, how to best make those shots, and the conditions that will allow you to make them. Anticipate where to be and what to do to get the results you want. Then, when you see opportunities while you are out there, you can quickly take full advantage of them.

Finally, and perhaps most importantly, in other types of photography you are an observer with a camera, without a part to play in whatever you are photographing. But in outdoor adventure photography, you are both a photographer and a participant in the adventure that you are photographing. This has an upside and a downside. On the upside, as a participant you get a unique perspective on your subject matter and often are inspired by your emotional engagement with the adventure itself and with your companions. But on the downside, you have to focus not only on taking pictures but also on climbing the peak, running the rapids, skiing from one hut to the next, or doing whatever activity you are engaged in. It can be tough to do both well—and sometimes dangerous. To compound the problem, most adventures include other people who are not photographers and often will not have the patience for those who are. So be sure to find a safe balance between your participation in the adventure, your companions, and your photography—one that ensures you enjoy all three.

GREAT PHOTOGRAPHS VS. SNAPSHOTS

What makes a great photograph and how do you make the transition from casual snapshooter to serious photographer? A good photograph does a good technical job of recording places and events. However, a great photograph goes beyond mere recording to create an image that expresses a message or theme about your world or experiences and captures a unique instance on film in which all the elements of photography come together. Thus, before you can make a great photograph, you must know what it is that you want to express in your photographs and become engaged with the world around you so you will see the opportunities to create that expression on film.

A great photograph starts with a strong composition made at the decisive moment that best captures the essence of what you want to express. Then add light with the right character, which can transform even the most mundane subject into a unique image. Next, correctly expose the film to transfer the image that you have created onto film, using that film as both a creative and a recording medium. Finally, use your equipment as a tool kit, using each of your kit's components to its fullest capability, paying close attention to all the details that result in that great photograph.

There are a number of things that you must do, which occur more or less in tandem over time, to make the transition from snapshooter to serious photographer. Like anything worth doing, it takes an investment of time and energy. First, you have to figure out what you want to photograph. What is it about your world and your experiences that you want to record? What images do you want to create and what themes or messages should those images communicate?

To be really creative, you must learn to see your subjects and the light illuminating them. A first glance or casual look may reveal a photo opportunity, but not the best image. To see that, you must visually ex-

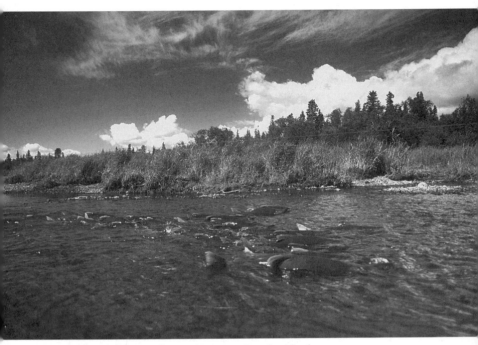

Spawning Sockeye Salmon, Hansen Creek, Alaska

plore both the subject and the light and learn to see the graphic designs that the two create. Seeing through your own eyes, however, is not enough. You have to learn to see the world as your camera does—which is different from how you see it—and then visualize images as the camera sees them. Once you can do this, your camera becomes a creative extension of your mind and emotions and not just a recorder.

It is also important to develop a personal style that shows your subjects, themes, and stories in your own creative way. This requires taking lots of pictures, gaining experience in how your camera works, and experimenting to see what you like. You can also read photography magazines and books, such as this one, as well as books on graphic design and composition. Look at the work of other photographers in magazines and books on travel, adventure, outdoor recreation, and natural history that emphasize photography, such as *National Geographic*, as well as posters, calendars, and galleries. Study the photographs that you like to understand why you like them and analyze how the photograph was made. Try applying what you learn from these to your own photography.

Finally, master the technical side of photography while exploring the artistic side by learning from books such as this one as well as getting lots of practice. Cameras, lenses, film, and all the other gadgets that fill our bags are only tools. Like any other tools, they do not do anything by themselves. To make great photographs, you have to put them to good use. Learn all the features of your camera, how your different lenses see things, how your film behaves, and when to use the various accessories that complement your camera. With practice and experimentation, you will ultimately settle on a way of using your tools to create the images that you want. When it becomes second nature to use your gear, you can really have fun, make the most of your photo opportunities, and take photographs that you may not even be able to imagine today.

WHO IS THIS BOOK FOR?

This book is for camera-carrying adventurers who want to bring back great photographs from their adventures, ones to hang on the wall, include in slide shows, and perhaps even publish. It is primarily for backpackers, paddlers, skiers, climbers, travelers, and other adventurers who carry cameras in the pursuit of adventure and who want to go beyond simply pointing and shooting, to learn to create images that capture the essence of their experience and the world around them. But it is also for serious photographers who hike, paddle, ski, climb, or travel to pursue the adventure of photography and who also want to get the best shots on such trips. Whether your adventures take you to backyard parks or exotic lands, whether you carry a simple point-and-shoot camera or a pack full of sophisticated camera gear, this book can help you bring back great shots—ones that let you relive your experience and evoke a "wish I was there" or "wow" in the rest of us.

This book is for users of all 35mm cameras, from compact point-and-shoots with a fixed lens to more sophisticated, professional-level single-lens reflex (SLR) cameras. The latter provide much more creative control and flexibility, which make it easier to return with the kinds of photographs that you want. Some types of photography, such as high-speed action, wild animal portraits, or macro, are only possible with more sophisticated gear. Each chapter of this book is filled with a variety of ideas and tips that take full advantage of the control and flexibility that such cameras provide.

However, in most cases a full set of bells and whistles is not absolutely necessary to make great images. You can take great photographs with a pocket-sized point-and-shoot camera, also called a lens-shutter camera, by making full use of what you can control. Because creating a strong composition and finding the right light are independent of camera type, the first two chapters can help you make better pictures with even the simplest of cameras. The third and fourth chapters, on exposure and gear, can provide some help, depending on how much control you have over the camera and the accessories that can be used with it. The final chapter, especially its first half, can also help the point-and-shoot user when it comes to putting it all together in the field.

This book is also for users of both completely manual and fully automatic cameras. With a manual camera, or with the manual mode provided on some automatic cameras, you have complete control over variables like shutter speed, aperture, and film speed. This control is great for creativity, but can be inconvenient and time consuming. Sometimes you miss great shots while fumbling with the camera. This book helps you take full advantage of this control and provides a variety of ways to make manual cameras easier to use.

Automatic cameras, on the other hand, choose the settings for some or all of these variables for you, which makes them quick and easy to use but often provides much less control, if any, over those variables. This book helps you understand what choices the camera makes so you can make the best use of the camera and take full advantage of what control you do have.

HOW TO USE THIS BOOK

This book is filled with a wealth of information and proven tips that will help just about any adventurer take more satisfying photographs. The first chapter covers composition, the art of creating an engaging, high-impact image that begins with your vision and ends with the photograph itself. The second chapter discusses the character of light, how to find the best light for the image you want, and how to make the most of the light you do have. The third chapter reviews how to measure the light and determine the exposure that gives you the shot you want.

The fourth chapter helps you get the most out of your camera gear and describes a variety of key accessories that will complement your camera system, producing better photographs. The final chapter brings these four elements together with a variety of tips and ideas for getting better shots while adventuring, including how to take better people, action, scenic, close-up, and wildlife photographs.

Photography can be impenetrably technical, which keeps many people from becoming better photographers. However, the more you understand about the technology, the more artistic you can be and, ultimately, the better pictures you can take. This book is full of suggestions that make the technology easier to use, or at least keep it from getting in your way. To make it as easy as possible, we have minimized the use of technical terminology and jargon. Where we have used such terms, we have defined them as simply as possible. Terms that are used repeatedly throughout the book are italicized when first used and also defined in the glossary at the back of the book. If you do not know the meaning of a term, then refer to the glossary.

Unlike other books that sit on the shelf once you have scanned the pictures, this one is meant to be taken along with your camera. Read it through; then toss it in your pack or camera bag and use it to make the most of your adventurous photo opportunities. It can serve as a reference when you cannot remember things like the proper exposure compensation for a particular situation, it can provide hints that might help you get the best possible photograph, and it can even give you some ideas on shots to take while on your adventures.

Because this book is meant to be taken along as a reference, and thus had to be kept light, it does not cover the fundamentals of how cameras work. With all the different types and brands of cameras available today, it would be impossible to include discussion on all the different models that the diverse readers of this book might have. So the book assumes that you understand the basics of how your camera works and the particular features that it has. If this is not the case, then review your camera's manual before reading this book. If you want to fully understand how to do something suggested in the book with your particular camera, then consult your owner's manual as you read along. Even better, also have your camera handy to try things as you read about them. Most owner's manuals are relatively small; you might want to take both your manual and this book along on your trips.

As a last note before you dive into the book: use your camera to explore your world and enhance the experience of adventure, but do so safely, keeping your eyes and mind open. Good shooting!

ACKNOWLEDGMENTS

The authors wish to thank Dona Reed, Heather Paxson, Carl Skoog, Ray Pfortner, and Chris Eckhoff for their help and support in writing this book.

Chapter 1

COMPOSITION

Composition is the act of creating an engaging image, one that reaches out and grabs the viewer—or at least piques his or her interest. Regardless of what kind of camera you use, composition is the key to your transition from making snapshots to making high-impact photographs. A strong composition is elegantly simple yet filled with just the right amount of energy to involve the viewer. It evokes an emotional reaction or communicates a single message and can overcome most technical imperfections.

Composition is an active process that begins with determining your purpose in taking the picture and ends with pressing the shutter release button. In between, you decide what to include in the picture, what to eliminate, and how to arrange the remaining elements to best suit your purpose. This chapter shows you how to use this process to create more satisfying photographs with any type of camera.

ELEMENTS OF COMPOSITION
Emphasize the Subject
The process of composing a photograph starts with the subject. Good composition must have a clear subject, center of interest, or theme, which could be as obvious as a charging grizzly bear or as subtle as the chill of a winter landscape. The lack of a subject is the primary cause of boring or confusing photographs that leave your viewers wondering why you bothered to take the picture or, worse, why you bothered to show it to them.

Once you have settled on what the subject is, do not be too quick to point-and-shoot. Rather, take some time to really see and analyze. Ask yourself what it is about that subject that you like. What is it that you want to capture on film? What is the message that you want to convey? What reaction do you want to evoke from anyone viewing this photograph? Many aspects of a subject or scene can be appealing. Some are obvious, like the exuberant faces of your climbing companions, the mystic beauty of an ancient temple, the power of a charging elephant, or the elegance of a great egret in breeding plumage. However, other subjects are more subtle, like the textures of lichen-covered rocks, the patterns of color in a flower-filled meadow, the rhythms of the grain in weathered wood, the sublime colors of sunrise over a misty lake, or the flowing shapes of water-sculpted rocks. These take more time to see, but taking that time is critical to effective composition.

Keeping in mind your subject and what aspects of it you want to capture, you can now begin the process of eliminating everything that detracts from it and maximizing the visual impact of your photograph.

Eliminate Distractions

Several frequently encountered distractions can easily compromise an image that otherwise is quite powerful, but they are easily avoided. These distractions, which you of course did not notice at the time, have a mysterious way of appearing in your photograph's background. Unfortunately, they can be visual magnets that can draw the viewer's attention away from the subject.

A camera does not "see" the way the human eye sees. This limitation, if understood and managed thoughtfully, can be used to your creative advantage. If not, it results in distractions that can ruin an otherwise good photograph.

When you look at your subject, you tend to see what is important to you. Your mind subconsciously filters what your eyes record, eliminating all the extraneous material and emphasizing the subject. When you view a burst of spring wildflowers, you see their beauty. You often do not see the surrounding weeds, the dead sticks beyond, the odd wilted petal, or the one bug-eaten leaf that would detract from that beauty—unless you really look for them.

Your camera, on the other hand, records everything contained in the viewfinder. No matter how expensive or automatic, whether a fancy single-lens reflex (SLR) or a simple point-and-shoot (also called a lens-shutter camera), a camera cannot do what your brain does. It will see the wildflowers—dead sticks, wilted petals, bug-eaten leaves, and all. The resulting picture may show the beauty that you saw, but often it is lost among a visual jumble that will leave you wondering why you wasted the film. For the camera to see what you saw or what you want it to see, you have to consciously emphasize what is important to you and eliminate everything else. To compose an effective photograph, you must simplify the visual chaos that surrounds you.

Your camera also has a much more limited ability to record a scene than you do. Film records a more narrow range of tones than your eyes can see, which means that in your photographs shadows may appear to be much darker, sometimes black, and highlights much brighter, sometimes white, than you remember seeing them. Film may also record colors differently than you see them, sometimes rendering them warmer, cooler, or brighter, which can have a subtle but significant impact on your photograph.

Your eyes see in three dimensions, but a camera produces flat, two-dimensional images, which means that objects that were behind your subject may appear to be part of the subject. Photographs compress what you saw in three-dimensional space to a two-dimensional plane. Consequently, more distant objects within a scene may appear to merge with closer objects in your photograph. For example, a dark moose may get lost in the dark hillside that was several hundred yards behind it, or a sapling 20 to 30 feet beyond the animal may appear to be growing out of its head. This is a problem especially common in pictures taken with *telephoto lenses*, which compress the spatial relationships between objects in the scene. You often will not see these distracting, and sometimes confusing, merges unless you look for them. Use your position to clearly separate important objects in your photograph, especially the subject from any potentially confusing objects that are behind it.

ELIMINATING DISTRACTIONS

- **Get subject sharply focused**
- **Keep background out of focus**
- **Look for background highlights and merges**
- **Sweep edges of frame**

Your eyes focus virtually everything they see, but your camera can have a much more limited area that is in focus—or *depth of field* (see Aperture, chapter 3)—which means that some part of your photograph may be out of focus. Small points of light in an otherwise dark background become large, distracting highlights when the background is out of focus. The worst offenders are light reflected from drops of water and the sky peeking out of small gaps between leaves in dense forest canopy or other dark objects. The *contrast* limitations of film compound the problem. Areas in the background that seemed only a bit lighter when you took the photograph often appear bright white in your photograph.

Other background objects that are not quite in focus detract from the subject because your viewer tries to put them in focus and figure out what they are. People's faces are especially bad because your viewer will wonder who they are rather than appreciate the intent of your photograph. Try a larger *aperture*, as discussed later in this chapter, to blur any objects in the background that might become distracting merges.

In addition, your camera records only a slice of what you can actually see, bounded by the four edges of your viewfinder. You have to make decisions about what to include inside those edges and what to exclude, as well as think about how these edges themselves interact with what you left inside them.

An object that is partially in the picture, cut off by the edge of the *frame*, can be distracting. Your viewer will wonder what it is and if it is supposed to be in the picture or not. Either put enough of the object in the frame to make it instantly recognizable or eliminate it completely. This simple guideline is complicated by the fact that the viewfinders of most cameras show only 90 percent to 95 percent of what will actually be captured in your photograph. Consequently, things may appear in your picture that you did not see in the viewfinder. Consult your owner's manual for the percentage that your viewfinder shows in both the horizontal and vertical directions. Then factor this in when composing an image.

Avoiding these distractions is easy if you take the time. When photographing we tend to focus both our lenses and our eyes on the subject, often ignoring the rest of what is in the viewfinder. To avoid unintended distractions, pay as much attention to the background and edges as you do the subject.

Before pressing the shutter-release button, check the entire image by looking beyond the subject and sweeping the edges of your viewfinder with your eyes. If your camera has one, use your *depth-of-field preview button*. Try to imagine what the scene in your viewfinder will look like in your photograph. Look for shadows and highlights that will become distractingly black and glaringly white on film, as well as for unintended edge effects and merges. The corrections are usually as simple as moving a few feet or opening up the aperture one *f-stop*. But you have to see the distractions to be able to avoid them. So slow down, take your time, and your composition will improve dramatically.

Maximize Visual Impact

The key to effective composition is to quickly pull the viewer into the photograph with something of interest, then keep the viewer there with just enough tension, energy, or movement to keep the mind and emotions working. Too little of these results in a static image that can create some impact if the subject itself is of interest. Too much results in a confusing image that can drive viewers away from the photograph.

Sometimes the subject itself may be so spectacular that just doing a good job of isolating it is sufficient. Even a bad shot of a visitor from outer space emerging from its spaceship should grab all but the most numbed viewer. More often, the subject may get attention, but something more is needed to create impact.

Simplicity. Most importantly, simplify the image. If you are shooting a portrait of a bugling elk, then fill the frame with him and eliminate everything else. If you are shooting a big scene, then only include enough to tell the story as simply as possible, nothing more. The impact of many images is lost because there is too much going on in the photograph. Incorporate only the subject and parts of a scene that enhance the subject and eliminate everything else.

Size. Size alone can grab attention. Fill the frame as much as possible by moving closer, zooming in, or switching to a longer lens. A tiny subject can get lost in the rest of the picture no matter how exciting it is. But be careful of filling the frame so much that the viewer loses all sense of scale or place. Often it is better to leave something else in the image to show how big or small the subject is, or to leave enough of the surroundings to show the subject in a context that makes it even more meaningful.

MAXIMIZING VISUAL IMPACT

+ **Choose a clear subject**
+ **Simplify the image**
+ **Fill the frame**
+ **Look for background contrast**

Contrast. Contrast can make your subject really stand out from the rest of the image. Lighter-toned, brighter-colored objects tend to come forward in a photograph, while darker objects tend to recede. Thus, a bright, well-lit subject is best shown against a darker background as shown in Plate 2. The reverse, in which you have a dark silhouette against a bright background as in Plate 1, also works and is great for showing shapes. Other types of contrast can also be effective. Rougher textures stand out from a smoother background, as does a warm subject against a cool background, an in-focus subject against an unrecognizably blurred background as in Plate 3, or a unique object against a uniform background such as the zebras in Plate 4.

19

Use your position to create contrast by placing your subject, or the most important parts of your image, against a contrasting background. To be dramatically darker than the subject on film, the background does not have to look dramatically darker than the subject to you. Just placing a well-lit subject against a background that is in the shadows is sufficient. Use your *light meter* to take readings from both the subject and the background to find enough difference to make the subject really stand out (see chapter 3).

Color. Color itself is also important. Bright colors, especially the primaries—red, yellow, and blue—create more excitement and energy and tend to come forward in a photograph. More muted pastels and earth tones have a quieter, more relaxing effect and tend to recede. Mixing colors together with or against their complement—red with green, orange with blue, and yellow with purple—enhances the effect of color. For example, the visual impact of a scarlet macaw in Plate 5 and the wildflowers in Plate 7 is quite striking.

TECHNIQUES TO ENHANCE COMPOSITION

Once you understand the elements of composition—emphasizing the subject, eliminating everything that detracts from it, and maximizing the visual impact of your photograph—you are ready to begin the process of composition. This process involves deciding where to position your camera, what lens length to use, what *shutter speed* and aperture to use, and how to arrange the elements in the viewfinder, and, finally, pressing the shutter release button.

Position Your Camera

Find the perspective that best shows your subject and eliminates distractions. Do not just take your picture from the first spot where you noticed your subject without first trying other camera positions.

Point of view. Move closer to make the subject bigger in your viewfinder, perhaps filling the frame so there is no doubt what the subject is. Or back away so the subject and part of its surroundings are also included, to tell a more complete story—but not too far. Many otherwise good compositions are weakened by the subject's being just too small. Move around to determine what camera position relative to the subject works best. Or, if the subject is active, wait for it to move into the best position. Use the camera's position relative to the subject to select the best light and background, as well as to eliminate any distractions that might detract from the subject or, worse, compete with the subject itself for your viewers' attention. Look before you shoot. Often, just moving a few feet can mean the difference between a mediocre snapshot and an attention-grabbing image.

For example, if you want to photograph a doe and fawn grazing at the edge of a small, wooded pond, should you position yourself across the pond from the animals to capture their reflection? Or should you position the deer between you and the water so the water provides an attractive backdrop? Which position is better depends upon which photograph you want. The first position might be better if you want a photograph of a wooded scene in which the deer and their reflections are only a part of that scene. The second position might be better if you want a portrait of the deer themselves. Either way, you get a different picture depending on where you position your camera.

Angle of view. In addition to your position, also consider the angle of view. Simply shooting at eye level, which is most commonly done, may not always work best. Changing the angle of view may create a much more interesting composition. For different effects, try shooting down on the subject for a bird's-eye view or up on the subject for a bug's-eye view. Climbing trees and crawling on the ground can result in unique shots. People are not used to viewing subjects from these perspectives; thus, they can be very effective in getting your viewer's attention. But be careful; such views can also be disconcerting if they are too different from reality or your viewer's expectations.

COMPOSITION CHECKLIST

+ **Select your subject or theme**
+ **Best camera position?**
+ **Lens focal length?**
+ **Aperture for needed depth of field?**
+ **Shutter speed to show or freeze motion?**
+ **Vertical or horizontal format?**
+ **Position subject within the frame**
+ **Check background and edges for distractions**
+ **Wait for the decisive moment**

Always analyze the possibilities before you start shooting. Move around, looking through your viewfinder, to find the perspective that works best. Try different positions and angles for different effects. No one point of view is correct, but one may be better than another to get the photograph that you want.

Choose Your Lens Length

Lens *focal length* can have a big impact on composition by determining what is included within your photograph and how objects appear relative to each other.

Normal. So-called *normal lenses*, those around 50mm in focal length for a 35mm camera, record a scene much as do your eyes. The relative sizes of objects and the spatial relationships between them look about the same way you would see them.

Wide angle. Lenses with a shorter focal length, in the 15mm to 35mm range, referred to as *wide-angle lenses*, provide a broader view and are used to tell a story or record a bigger scene with a foreground and a background. They create a sense of expansiveness and openness by increasing the apparent distance between objects in the scene. They create a sense of depth by exaggerating the convergence of lines as they recede into the background and by making foreground objects appear larger and background objects relatively smaller. Wide-angle lenses also provide greater depth of field (see Depth of Field, chapter 4), which allows much more of a scene to be in focus. Wide angles are great for showing a subject in the foreground in the context of its background surroundings, as in Plate 6 with the moose antler in the foreground and Alaskan peaks in the distance.

Telephoto. Lenses with a longer focal length, referred to as telephoto lenses, magnify the subject and provide a narrower view, which isolates a single object or a small part of a bigger scene. They compress the space between elements in the scene, resulting in flatter but more intimate compositions. Their apparent decrease in depth of field is ideal for creating an in-focus subject against a background that is out of focus, such as the deer in Plate 3.

Telephotos with midrange focal lengths, in the 75mm to 150mm range for a 35mm camera, are ideal for tighter shots of a single subject, especially people. They can isolate the subject without too much compression while maintaining a comfortable distance from the subject.

Telephotos with longer focal lengths, 200mm or greater, are ideal for taking a small slice out of a big scene or emphasizing a subject toward which you cannot move any closer. Their narrow field of view eliminates surrounding distractions and isolates the subject. Their compression of space makes distant objects seem very close to the ones in front, which can create some very interesting effects. For example, if you photograph trekkers viewing dramatic peaks in the distance with a telephoto lens, the peaks appear to loom over them, as in Plate 1, when in fact the peaks might be quite far away. With a wide-angle lens, the peaks would appear to be much farther away and much less dramatic.

However, this compression can result in distracting merges that can ruin an otherwise great shot. For example, a branch or tree far beyond a bear you are photographing may appear to be growing right out of its head in the resulting image. Or objects well beyond your subject that are about the same tone or color may look like they are part of the subject, resulting in a confusing image. Look for potential distractions behind your subject. With a telephoto's narrow field of view, even a slight shift in your position can eliminate them.

When photographing your subject, try different lenses or different focal lengths of your *zoom lens*, which combines a range of focal lengths into one lens. You can make very different yet equally effective compositions of the same subject from the same vantage point simply by shooting with a variety of lenses or focal lengths. For example, you could capture the essence of a flower-filled meadow in a variety of ways by shooting with different lenses. If you want to tell a story by showing the beauty of the meadow's flowers in the context of the meadow and surrounding scenery, as in Plate 7, select a wide-angle lens. If you want to show a slice of the meadow with its patchwork of color, as in Plate 8, select a telephoto. These represent the two ends of focal-length choices. Between these extremes lie subtle differences that can make for better photographs.

Choose Your Exposure

Exposure choices can also make a big impact on composition. A variety of aperture and shutter-speed combinations can provide the correct exposure (see chapter 3). Thus, the particular aperture and shutter speed you select should be primarily dictated by their effects on composition. Careful selection of aperture and shutter speed provides a lot of creative control that you can use to your advantage.

Aperture determines depth of field or how much of your photograph is in focus (see chapters 3 and 4), and shutter speed determines the effect of motion in your photograph. When you want to control depth of field, first select the aperture that provides the depth of field that you want; then set the shutter speed or, if you have an automatic camera, use *Aperture Priority Mode* (in which you select the aperture and your camera selects the appropriate shutter speed) to get the exposure that you want. When the effect of motion is more important, first select the shutter speed; then set the aperture or use *Shutter Priority Mode* (in which you select the shutter speed and your camera selects the appropriate aperture). If neither is more important than the other, first set the aperture to f/8 or f/11 (see chapter 3), then set the shutter speed, or use *Program Mode* (in which the camera selects both aperture and shutter speed).

Aperture. Wide apertures, f/5.6 and bigger, result in a relatively shallow depth of field with the subject in focus against a blurred background. These apertures are ideal for isolating an object or small piece of a scene.

To best emphasize the subject, the background should be a different color or tone than the subject. For example, a well-lit subject in front of a darker, blurred background really stands out, as does the deer in Plate 3. However, be careful of background highlights. Little spots of light that do not look like much to you will become big, distracting hot spots in an out-of-focus background. Use your depth-of-field preview button, if your camera has one, to check for these (see Depth of Field, chapter 4).

Narrow apertures, f/16 and smaller, result in a much deeper depth of field, sometimes extending to infinity. These apertures are ideal for telling a story or packing a lot of information into an image, such as big landscapes in which you want both the foreground and background to be in focus, as in Plate 6. Unfortunately, small apertures dictate slower shutter speeds, which may require use of a tripod or some other camera support to ensure a sharp photograph.

Managing depth of field is a balancing act. The aperture should be wide enough so that all the important parts of your photograph are in focus. Key parts of the image that are not in focus may be distracting and diminish the impact of the photograph. On the other hand, depth of field should be narrow enough to put the unimportant parts of the scene, especially in the background, out of focus, thus isolating what is most important. A background that is in focus may draw your viewer's attention away from the subject. Use the depth-of-field preview button on your camera or *depth-of-field scale* on your lens before shooting to check the depth of field, *opening up* or *stopping down* the aperture as needed to get the right amount (see Depth of Field, chapter 4).

Shutter speed. Fast shutter speeds, 1/125 second or faster, freeze the motion of the subject, camera, or both in most situations. Freezing the motion of very fast-moving subjects, such as downhill skiers or cyclists at full speed, may require even faster speeds. Slower shutter speeds record motion as a blurring of the subject if it is moving, or a blurring of the entire picture if the camera is moving. Eliminating this blurring when using slower shutter speeds requires the use of a tripod or other camera support (see Eliminating Camera Movement, chapter 4). Whether you show your subject's motion as an instant captured in time or a blur of implied motion as the subject whizzes by depends on your purpose and is covered in the next section.

Capture Action and Motion

There are three ways to show action or motion in your photographs.
Freezing motion. The first technique is to use very fast shutter speeds to freeze the subject's motion, as in the photograph of the breach-

ing whale in Plate 9. This might be most effective for subjects for which you want to show facial expressions, straining muscles, or a unique instant in time, such as a kayaker cresting a waterfall, a skier turning on a gate, or a grizzly bear fishing for salmon. Anticipation is the key to getting this type of shot, especially with the high-speed action of a flying bird or a running animal. If you can see the moving subject in your viewfinder, you have probably missed the shot, especially if the subject is relatively close to you. You actually have to press the shutter release button just before or just as the subject enters the viewfinder.

Stopping very fast subjects such as skiers or a flying bird requires shutter speeds of 1/500 second or faster. Even faster shutter speeds, 1/1000 second or higher, may be required when the subject is close, accelerating rapidly such as a bird taking flight, or moving perpendicular to you. Slower speeds, 1/60 or 1/125 second, can be used when the subject is moving toward or away from you and is relatively far away. When in doubt, use the fastest shutter speed possible. Table 1-1 provides guidelines for different subject speeds and directions of movement. With automatic cameras, use Shutter Priority Mode, selecting a fast shutter speed, and let the camera pick the right aperture.

Table 1-1. Minimum Shutter Speeds to Freeze Motion*

	Direction of Movement		
	↓	↘	➡
Subject Speed	**Shutter Speed**		
Slow speed: walking, paddling, X-country skiing	1/60	1/125	1/250
Medium speed: jogging, trotting, bike touring	1/125	1/250	1/500
High speed: running, flying, downhill skiing	1/250	1/500	1/1000

*These guidelines are for a subject 25 to 30 feet away from you. If the subject is 10 to 15 feet away, double the speeds; if the subject is 50 to 60 feet away, cut them in half.

Blurring motion. The second approach is to slow the shutter down to capture an impression of motion itself, like the blur of the water as it runs over the stationary rocks in Plate 10. Shutter speeds of 1/15 second or slower blur the subject's motion and are effective ways to show the explosion of birds taking to the air, the speed of a running animal, or the graceful flow of a waterfall. When using this approach, be sure to use a

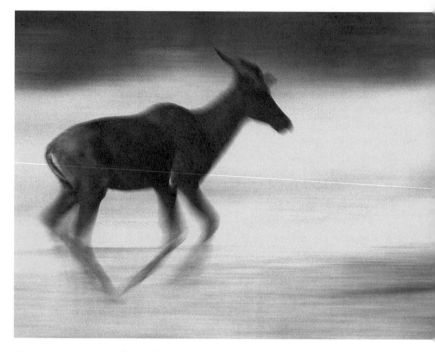

Figure 1-1 Tssessebe, Okavango River, Botswana

shutter speed slow enough to significantly blur the motion. If the subject is only slightly blurred, then you have a bad picture. In these types of shots, the boundary between subject and background is also harder to discern. So be careful not to lose the subject in the background; look for one that will make the subject stand out. If possible, use a solid tripod so camera movement does not cause blurring in unwanted directions.

Panning action. The last approach is *panning* or tracking the action with your camera rather than holding it still, as in Figure 1-1. While you follow the moving subject with your camera, depress the shutter release button as you move with the subject. In the resulting photograph, the subject will appear relatively sharp and the background blurred, implying that the subject is whizzing by the viewer. Try shutter speeds of about 1/30 to 1/2 second and use a tripod to track the subject's direction of movement without camera wobble. The faster shutter speed freezes the subject against a blurred background, whereas the slower shutter speeds also blur the animal. Panning works best when the subject is moving perpendicular to the camera.

Choose a Vertical or Horizontal Format

Once you've framed your subject by finding the best camera position, lens focal length, and exposure, you must choose either a horizontal or a vertical orientation for the frame. The 35mm frame is actually a 24mm by 36mm rectangle. A horizontal format orients the rectangle with the long axis running from left to right, while the vertical format orients it with the long axis running up and down. Which orientation you choose can affect the final image. For example, in Plate 1, the peak might not seem to loom so high over the trekkers had the image been shot in a horizontal format.

The horizontal format emphasizes the horizontal axis, creating a sense of width or depth. It is ideal for big landscapes, travel shots in which you have a person looking into the scene, and action shots in which there is horizontal movement. The vertical format, on the other hand, emphasizes the vertical axis, creating a sense of height. It is ideal for shots of trees, landscapes with a lot of elevation, and action shots in which the movement is up or down.

Do not shoot horizontals just because it is easier. Choose the orientation, vertical or horizontal, that best contributes to your composition. Select the orientation that best emphasizes the subject or theme of your photograph and eliminates any distractions. Or try both to create a different, but perhaps equally viable, image of the same subject.

Position the Subject in the Frame

The position of the subject or key parts of a scene within your photograph can also add to the impact of a composition. The center of the frame is often the weakest location, even though it is often most convenient to put your viewfinder's sights on the subject and fire away. Placement of the subject in the center can result in a static image, locking the viewer's eye into the middle with no place to go.

Likewise, placement of the subject too near the edges of the frame can be distracting and even confusing to the viewer. Avoid cramming the subject too close to an edge, especially if the rest of the image is full of other things that might also catch the viewer's attention. Avoid having the frame's edge cut off enough of an object that the viewer will wonder what it is and whether it is supposed to be in the picture. Avoid having a moving subject running into the frame's edge unless there is something very interesting behind the subject.

The positions with the most impact are off center but away from the edges. Imagine vertical and horizontal lines dividing the space within the

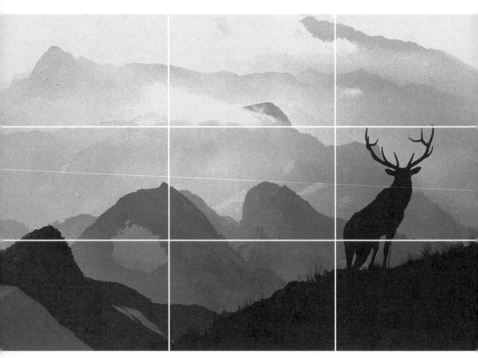

Figure 1-2 Elk, Banff National Park, Alberta, Canada

viewfinder roughly into thirds, as shown in Figure 1-2. The intersections of these grid lines represent the positions with the most visual interest, more dynamic than the center and less confusing than the edges. As a guideline, commonly referred to as the "Rule of Thirds" or the "Golden Mean," place your subject, such as the bears in Plate 11, or most important parts of the subject, such as the eyes of the wolf in Plate 2, at or near these intersections whenever possible. Place moving subjects at an intersection point, traveling into the frame.

    To create impact in a more complex photograph, incorporate paths for the viewer's eye to follow. These can support the subject, leading the viewer's eyes right where you want them to go, as do the cracks in the mud in Plate 12 or the tree trunks in Plate 25. They can also create movement between the key parts of a bigger scene, which adds a sense of depth, as shown in Figures 1-3 and 1-4. These paths can be explicit lines, such as the curves of a road, tree branches framing a peak, fences, stairways, or converging perspective lines. Or they can be implied, like the line along which people within the photograph are looking, a moving object's line of travel, a series of objects that recedes into the background, or lines that would connect important objects in a scene. But be careful with how you use these paths. They can detract from a composition as much as they can complement it. In particular, watch out for lines that lead the viewer out of the photograph unless something else is firmly anchoring the viewer into it.

In addition to providing paths for the eye to follow, lines can also have more subtle effects. Diagonal lines create a sense of tension or movement, whereas horizontal lines are more tranquil. Curves and curvy shapes imply fluidity and sensuousness, as in Figure 1-4. Simple shapes made from

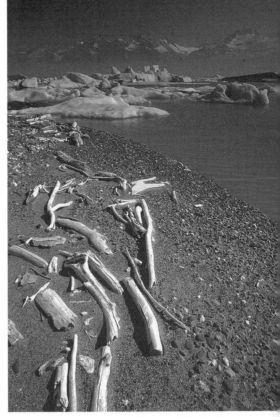

Figure 1-3 Bleached Driftwood, Alaska

diagonal lines, like triangles and diamonds, can add even more dynamism. Such lines or shapes can be explicit, but more often they are implied by the positions of objects within the photograph. Thus, two

Figure 1-4 Arctic Landscape, Canada

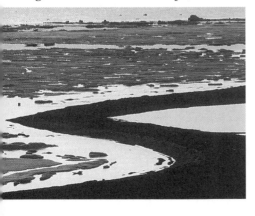

objects arranged along a diagonal line create more visual interest than if arranged horizontally. Three objects creating a triangle have even more impact, such as the triangle created by the eyes of the three penguins in Plates 14 and 15.

Other elements can be incorporated into your photograph to add to the impact you want to make. For example, bold colors are usually

29

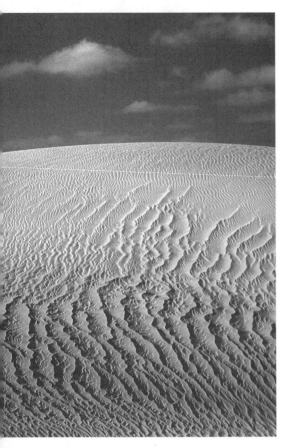

Figure 1-5 Sand Dunes, Australia

more evocative, with reds connoting heat or passion and blues connoting coolness or serenity, while soft pastel colors are more harmonious and subtle in their effect. Textures can add a sense of touch, allowing the viewer to "feel" the subject. Finally, patterns of lines or shapes can add appealing rhythms and interesting abstractions, as in Figures 1-5 and 1-6.

Capture the Decisive Moment

Just as the right camera position is important, sometimes the right moment in time can make the difference between a good snapshot and a powerful image. These moments, such as when a foraging bear lifts its head to look at you, a cyclist comes flying around a corner, or the rising sun bathes your subject in warm light, offer opportunities to capture something special in your photographs. To make the most of these opportunities, you have to be ready for them, especially when things are happening fast. Quick reactions as well as cameras with autofocus lenses and power winders can help, but decisive moments often happen too quickly for you to count on these alone to capture them.

Anticipating them is the key. Slow down to study your subject's movement, to watch what is going on around the subject, to analyze the play of the light. By waiting and watching, you develop a sense for what is about to happen and will more likely be ready for it when it does. Try to visualize the images you want, making compositional and technical decisions needed to make the photographs you want well ahead of time. Then be on the lookout for these images or the conditions that can create them and have your camera ready to shoot.

This anticipation is especially important when things are moving or changing quickly. For example, simply reacting to a fast-moving downhill skier, raising your camera, and pressing the shutter release button as he or she whizzes by you will most likely result in a great shot of the snow. At those speeds, if you can see the decisive moment in your viewfinder, you may well miss it in your photograph. However, if you watch the movement, position yourself before the skier gets to you, preset focus and exposure, and snap the picture just as the subject enters or is about to enter the frame, you will more likely get the shot.

As in finding the best position from which to shoot, do not just fire away. Rather, slow down, observe, and analyze. You will be much better able to pick the right time to get the most photograph. If the decisive moment does not happen when expected, just wait; it will.

*Figure 1-6 **Mountain Ridges, North Cascades, Washington***

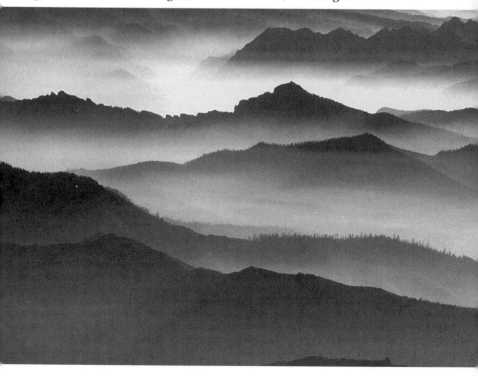

Chapter 2

NATURAL LIGHT

Light, of course, makes photography possible. Without it we could not enjoy the beauty and adventure of the outdoors, much less bring back pictures of our experiences. While there certainly has to be enough light to properly expose your film, it is the character, or quality, of the light that really makes the photograph. With the right light, rich in character, even a mundane subject can make an outstanding image. Learning to find the best light, to use what light you do have to your advantage, and even to not photograph in the wrong light are the next steps toward making better photographs. This chapter covers the characteristics of light to look for, as well as where and when to find them. The quantity of light needed to make a photograph is covered in chapter 3, Exposure.

In outdoor and adventure photography, light primarily comes from one source: the sun. Other sources, such as flash (see chapter 4), as well as fires, flashlights, or the moon (see chapter 5), can be used to augment sunlight and sometimes even replace it. These can create interesting effects, but their application is usually too limited and complicated for most outdoor adventures.

The light used to make a photograph travels from the sun through the earth's highly variable atmosphere, reflects off of the scene you are shooting (unless the sun itself is your subject), goes through your camera's lens, and finally hits the film in your camera. Along the way, the quality of the light is affected, sometimes dramatically, by its direction

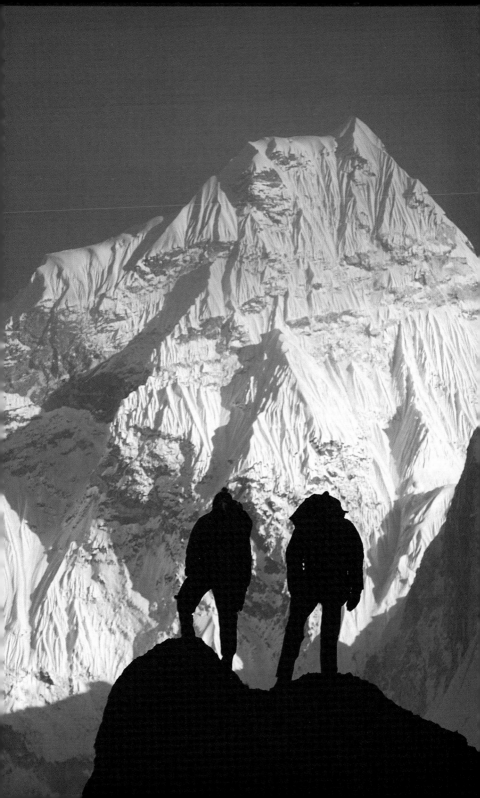

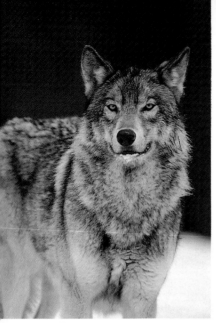
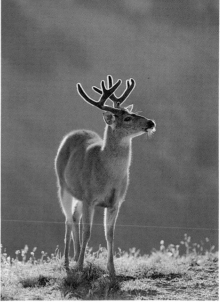

Plate 2 *Plate 3*

Plate 1 *overleaf:* Climbers, Ama Dablam, Nepal

Plate 2 Gray Wolf, Canada

Plate 3 Black-tailed Deer, Olympic National Park, Washington

Plate 4 Wildebeest and Zebras, Masai Mara, Kenya

Plate 4

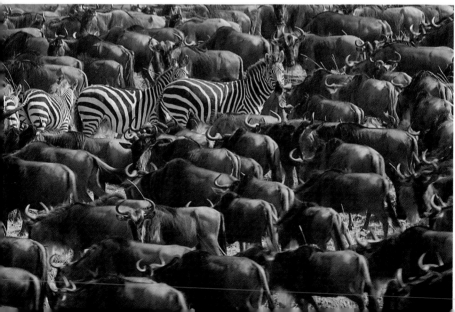

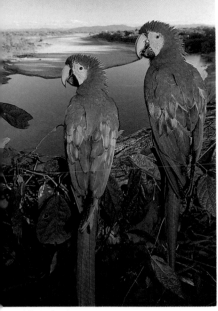

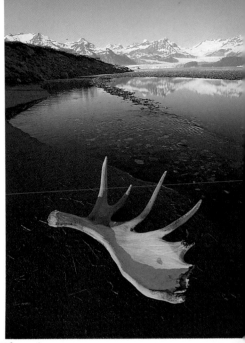

Plate 5

Plate 6

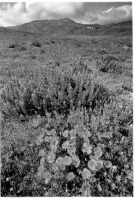

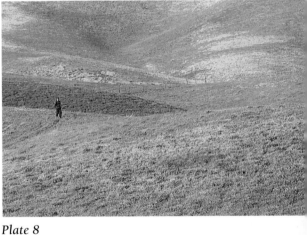

Plate 7

Plate 8

Plate 5 Scarlet Macaws, Tambopata River Region, Peru

Plate 6 Moose Rack, Alsek River, Alaska

Plate 7 Poppies and Lupine, Central Coast, California

Plate 8 Spring Landscape, Central Coast, California

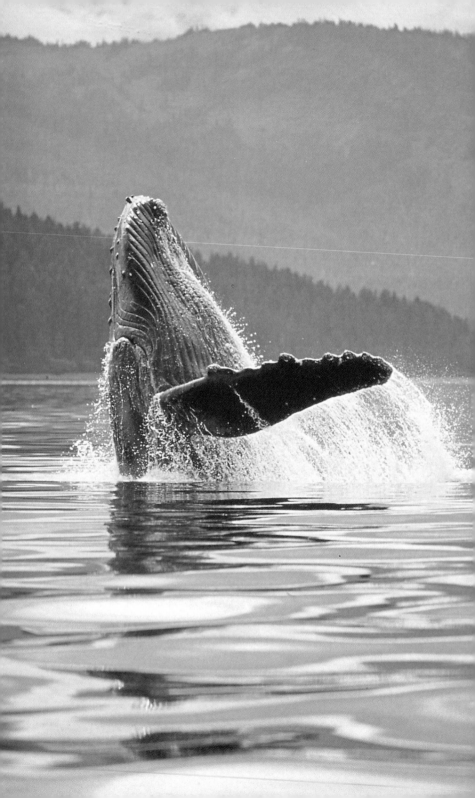

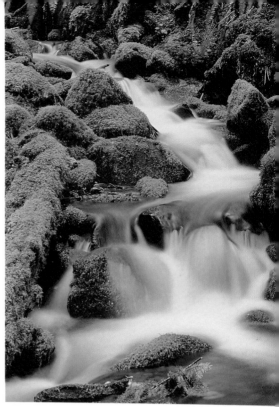

Plate 9 facing page:
Breaching Whale, Point
Adolphus, Alaska

Plate 10 Hoh Rain Forest,
Olympic National Park,
Washington

Plate 11 Brown Bears (Sow
and Cubs), Alaska

Plate 10

Plate 11

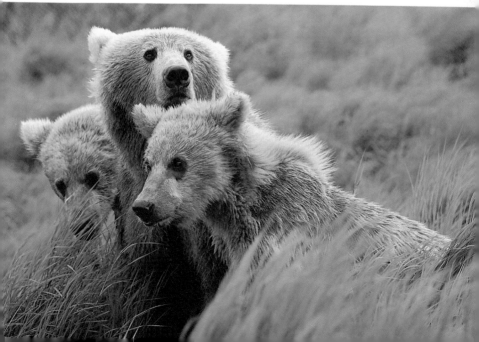

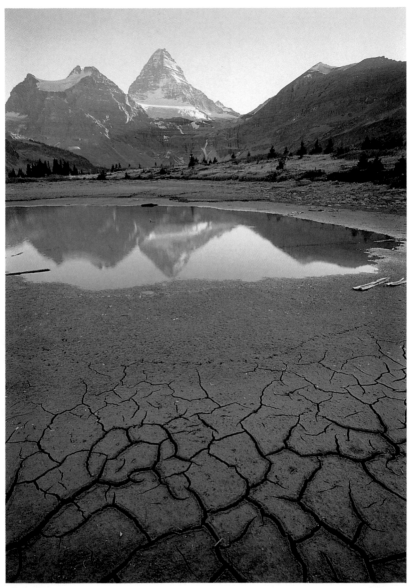

Plate 12

Plates 12 and 13 Mount Assiniboine Provincial Park,
Alberta, Canada

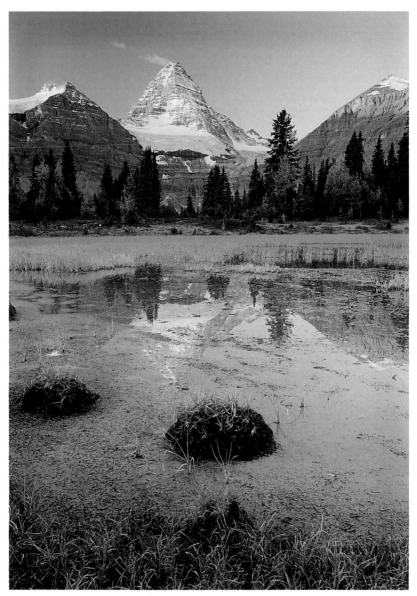

Plate 13

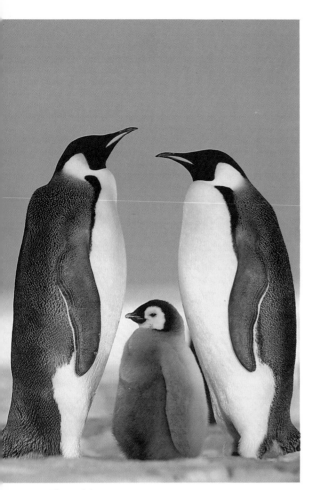

Plate 14

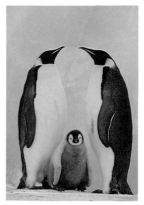

Plate 15

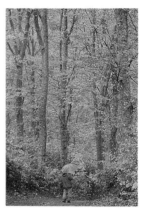

Plate 16

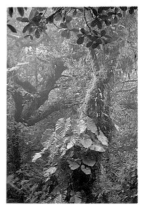

Plate 17

Plates 14 and 15 Emperor Penguins, Antarctica

Plate 16 Yaku-shima, Japan

Plate 17 Monteverde Cloud Forest Reserve, Costa Rica

8

relative to the subject, the time of day, any manipulation of the light that you might add, and even the film you use.

The light reflecting from a scene can be even or contrasty, bold or subdued, harsh or soft, warm or cool, as well as varying in color from red to blue. These characteristics evoke different emotional responses and create different moods, which you can use to enhance the impact of your photograph. For example, subdued, bluish light creates a more quiet, somber mood, as in Plate 12 and Plate 15; whereas bolder, warmer light creates more excitement and energy, as in Plate 13 and Plate 14. In general, the most appealing photographs are usually made in light that is more even but with enough contrast to add depth, not too bold, softer to take the hard edge off of shadows, and warmer with a hint of golden orange or red such as in Plate 13. Unfortunately, the right combination of characteristics does not just happen all the time.

To take advantage of the right light, you must first learn to see it. For most us, most of the time, light is the medium, not the message. Our brains tend to ignore the light per se and focus only on whatever it reveals. To become a better photographer, look not only at your subject but also at the light itself. Look for its various characteristics, paying attention to where and when you find them. Photograph similar subjects in different types of *natural light* to develop a sense for how light's character can affect your picures.

CONTRAST

Film records light differently than your eyes do. Consequently, film can change the light's character in the final image, sometimes enhancing the impact you want, sometimes detracting from it. Film can increase contrast, make colors more snappy or subdued, add warmth or coolness, change the color cast, and alter textures. Not only is it critical that you find the right light, but you must also understand how your film interacts with that light if you are to make better photographs. Experiment with different types of film to learn about these effects and what you like.

While contrast is a key to good photography, extreme contrast is one of the most common causes of bad photography. Contrast is simply the range of tones or brightness from the lightest (white) to the darkest (black). High contrast has a wide range of tones from deep, dark shadows to bright white highlights. Low contrast has a narrow range of tones without the extremes of dark shadows and highlights. Contrast is most extreme when the sun is high overhead on a summer day, especially inside forests or on snow and sand. Contrast is much less on overcast days or when the sun is very low in the sky, unless the scene you are shooting includes a lot of sky.

On a bright, sunny day when contrast is highest, you can usually see the full range of tones in a scene. You typically see the detail both in the shadows and in the bright highlights, unless you are looking right into the sun or you quickly look from one extreme to the other. Film, on the other hand, sees a much narrower range of tones than you can. It will not record the detail that you can see in either the shadows or the highlights, or in both. Consequently, little if any of what you could see in the scene's shadows or highlights will show up in your photograph. Rather, these will appear as unrecognizable black and white spaces that can weaken an otherwise good composition. Bright highlights in particular will draw your viewer's attention away from the subject. More subtly, soft edges will appear harder and more pronounced, which may obscure a subject's fine details and textures.

Even though some films can record more contrast than others, high contrast will overpower just about any film. If you can see dark, distinct shadows on a bright, sunny day, and you squint heavily when emerging from the shadows into the sun, then the contrast is probably too high for your film. For best results, keep contrast extremes and bright highlights out of your photographs. For example, if you are photographing a subject in the shadows on a sunny day, then eliminate the brightly lit areas from your viewfinder. Or wait for light that has less contrast, closer to the range that your film can record, and avoid the high contrast of midday when the sun is shining. Then you can use contrast to your advantage, instead of having it ruin your photographs.

DIRECT LIGHT

Direct light is, very simply, light that travels from the sun or other light source directly onto your subject without being significantly impacted along the way. *Indirect light*, on the other hand, illuminates your subject after being reflected and scattered by things like clouds, tree canopies, and even the atmosphere itself, which reflects light into open shadows. Direct light is typically more intense and harsher than indirect light, and its direction makes a significant impact on your photograph.

When photographing in direct light, do not simply follow the old adage of keeping the sun behind you and coming over your shoulder. Before shooting, look at other possibilities. Try different camera positions, so that the light source hits the subject from different directions, which can create very different images of the same subject. A saguaro cactus lit from the front makes an interesting image, but when it is lit from

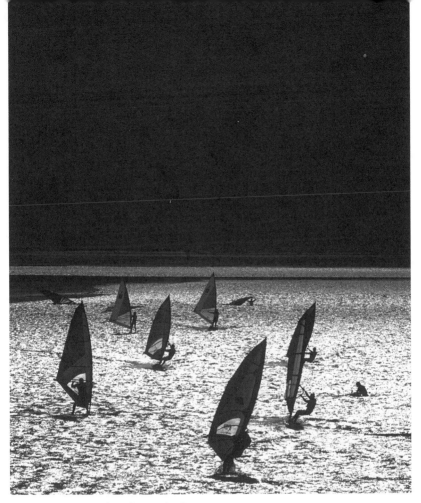

Figure 2-1 Windsurfers, Alaska

the side you can feel its sharp spines, and when it is lit from the back you
are also struck by its distinctive shape.

    Front-lighting. *Front-lighting*, in which the light source is in front of
the subject and behind the photographer, evenly lights your subject with
virtually no shadows. It is great for showing detail and color, as in Plate
14, but can produce flat images, because there are no shadows to add
depth and show textures.

    Sidelighting. *Sidelighting*, on the other hand, can produce much
richer images, as in Plates 6 and 13. Light coming in from either the left
or right of the subject casts shadows that define the shapes and textures
of an image. These shadows make photographs, which are inherently flat,
more three-dimensional with a greater sense of depth. They can create

stronger, more interesting graphic designs, adding more drama to the image. The textures that they reveal can add a tactile quality.

However, these shadows can also be distracting if contrast is too extreme, with what looked like soft shadows to your eyes becoming black holes in your photograph. Light coming from a direction of somewhere in between front- and sidelighting can be a good compromise, illuminating more of the subject but avoiding harsh shadows. Flash and reflectors (see chapter 4) can be used to fill in these shadows, which reduces the contrast to a range that film can record, often creating a more appealing photograph.

Backlighting. *Backlighting*, in which the light source is behind the subject and in the face of the photographer, is the trickiest to work with but can produce very dramatic images, as in Plate 3. While front-lighting fully illuminates a subject, leaving no shadows, backlighting has the opposite effect. It enhances contrast, creating silhouettes that emphasize your subject's shape. Backlighting can also surround your subject with a halo called rim lighting, adding a feeling of magic to your photograph. As with sidelighting, flash and reflectors can be used to light the front of your backlit subject, leaving it surrounded by this glowing rim light, often creating unique images (see chapter 4).

Top-lighting. *Top-lighting*, which occurs during midday when the sun is overhead, is the least appealing direction of light and is usually worth avoiding. Contrast is usually highest when the sun is directly overhead, often too high for film to record. Overhead light is typically very harsh and creates unappealing shadows on the faces of animals or people, often making them look like they have black eyes. As with front-lighting, top-lit photographs often look flat because there is little or no shadow to add depth to the scene.

Spotlighting. *Spotlighting* is a special type of direct lighting where a beam of light shines through clouds, forest canopy, or other opening to illuminate your subject, as it does the sailboat in Plate 24. Just as in theater, a single beam of light makes your subject stand out against darker surroundings, drawing attention to it. Look for spotlighting inside forests, during clearing storms, and in other conditions, especially when the sun is low in the sky, just after sunrise or before sunset. You can also create spotlighting on smaller subjects by using *fill flash* and underexposing the background (see chapter 4).

INDIRECT LIGHT

Indirect light can take on a range of characteristics, depending on how it is reflected or scattered as it travels to the subject. At one end of the spectrum, light reflecting from a mirror or other bright, reflective surface may be more like direct light in character, though somewhat less intense. If you see distinct shadows of objects lit by reflected light, which may occur on bright snow or sand, then treat the light as if it is direct light. However, if shadows are less distinct, then the light is indirect. At the other end of the spectrum, light shining through fog or clouds may be so scattered that by the time it reaches your subject, it is very diffuse, seeming to come from all directions and leaving no shadows at all.

Indirect light, found on overcast days and in shadows, illuminates your subject more evenly than direct light, creating no deep shadows or harsh highlights that may be distracting. Contrast is much lower than in direct light, allowing you to capture a more subtle range of tones and more detail in your subject. Indirect light is also much softer, eliminating the hard edges created by direct light. Colors are more saturated because there is no harsh glare to wash them out.

The clouds, fog, and precipitation that might otherwise keep you indoors can create ideal conditions for outdoor photography. The indirect, diffuse light found in such conditions often produces the most satisfying images, especially where you want to emphasize your subject's more subtle textures and details. It is great for close-ups and portraits as well as landscapes, if you minimize the amount of white sky in the picture. For example, the photographs of the poppy meadow in Plates 7 and 8, the bears in Plate 11, the Japanese scene in Plate 16, and the Costa Rican rain forest in Plate 17 were all taken on overcast days. These would have looked very differently taken under sunny skies; given the contrast limitations of film, they probably would not have even been worth taking.

However, indirect light also takes on the color of whatever it is reflecting off of and will subtly change the color of whatever it is illuminating. For example, the penguins in Plate 15 have a cool, blue cast because they are lit by sunlight reflecting off of blue ice. And the Kayapo mother and child in Plate 18 have a warm glow created by light reflecting off of the clay-colored ground in front of them. On overcast days, the light bounces off gray clouds and, consequently, takes on a cool, gray cast. Light in open shade on sunny days is reflected from the blue sky and takes on a cool, bluish cast.

Our eyes often do not see these color shifts until we get our pictures back. So look carefully for them when photographing in indirect light. Once you learn to see the changes, you can use them to create better photographs. For example, the photograph of the Kayapos in Plate 18 is far more appealing than one taken of them standing out in direct sunlight, which would have left dark shadows under their eyes. However, these

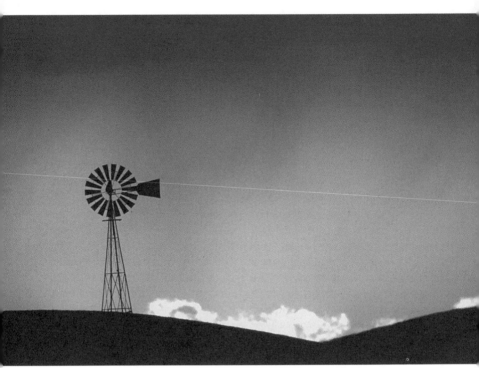

Figure 2-2 Windmill at Sunset, Palouse Region, Washington

changes can also detract from your photographs. If you want more natural-looking photographs, use different types of film and *filters* to counteract these changes (see chapter 4). For example, a *warming filter* would return the cool, blue penguins in Plate 15 to a more normal-looking color.

Indirect light also provides less light than direct sunlight, which may dictate the use of slower shutter speeds, a tripod, or faster film (see chapter 4).

ANGLE OF LIGHT/TIME OF DAY

When there are no clouds hiding the sun, the character of its light varies considerably throughout the day as the sun's angle relative to the horizon and its interaction with the earth's atmosphere change. Differences in the light's character divide the day roughly into six periods: before sunrise, the hour or so after sunrise, midday, the hour or so before sunset, after sunset, and night. The best times for photography on sunny days are generally during what photographers refer to as the *magic hours:*

the half hour or so before and after both sunrise and sunset.

Shooting at different times of day can result in photographs of the same subject that are quite different and that have different emotional impacts. For example, compare the photograph of Wonderlake and Denali (Plate 19) taken before the sunrise with the photograph of the same scene (Plate 20) taken much later in the day, or the photograph of Mount Assiniboine taken when the sun's last rays were striking the peak (Plate 12) with the shot of the same peak taken early in the day (Plate 13).

The length of each of these periods varies with latitude and season. At lower latitudes nearer the equator, sunrise and sunset come and go very quickly, so the periods when the light is best for photography are very short. The "magic hour" is reduced to the magic fifteen minutes. The sun stays overhead most of the day, creating a long midday period with harsh light and with too much contrast. At higher latitudes nearer the poles, the optimal periods before and after sunrise and sunset last far longer, at times almost all day. During summer, when the sun is much higher overhead, the periods of best light are also shorter. The light during most of the day is again harsh, with too much contrast. Nearer winter, as the angle of the sun recedes, these periods become much longer, reaching a peak in midwinter.

Before sunrise. During the period from the time the first rays of the sun begin to light the sky until just before the sun rises, the source of light for photography is not the sun itself but the sunlight being reflected from the sky. Thus, the light is indirect and very diffuse, with low intensity and contrast, but changing rapidly as the sun nears the horizon. Colors are softer and more pastel, although the sky may be awash in fantastic color or filled with flaming clouds, which makes for great landscapes (see Plate 19).

When the sun is still well below the horizon, long before sunrise, the light is relatively cool, with a bluish tint, as it reflects from a dark sky. As it nears the horizon, the light becomes warmer, with an orangish to pinkish tint, as the sky reddens. The sky itself is several f-stops brighter than the earth, which is great for shooting silhouettes, but may require the use of a *graduated neutral-density filter* (see chapter 4). Because light intensity is low, a slow shutter speed is necessary and a steady tripod and shutter release cable are a must (see chapter 4).

Hour after sunrise. After sunrise, from the time the sun first peeks over the horizon until an hour or so later, the sun's rays provide strong direct lighting at low angles, as in Plate 13, which is ideal for showing textures, creating strong graphic designs, and giving depth to your photographs. Light intensity is higher than before sunrise and increasing. Shutter speeds may not be as slow, although a tripod may still be needed. Contrast is still relatively low, usually within the film's range unless you include the sun in your photograph.

Because of the interaction of the low-angled light with the earth's atmosphere, the light at this time is much warmer, with a yellowish or reddish tint, and emotionally more appealing than at other periods of the day. Again, compare the emperor penguins in Plate 14 bathed in early morning light with the ones in shadow in Plate 15. Colors are much richer during this period than at other times of the day; reds and earth tones in particular may even seem to glow. Great light with relatively even contrast makes this an ideal time for just about any type of photography.

Midday. The worst time for photography is usually when the sun is high in the sky, unless a cloud cover is diffusing the harsh overhead light. The light is cooler, with a bluish tint, and colors are washed out by the sun's more intense glare. The light's direction—from the top—creates flat landscapes and casts unnatural shadows on faces. Contrast is more extreme, often exceeding the range that film can handle, resulting in distracting shadows and highlights in your photographs.

However, it is still possible to take good photographs during midday. You can simply avoid the harsh, direct top-light by shooting in the shadows, remembering to use a warming filter or warmer film (see chapter 4) to counteract the cool, bluish light found there. If no shadows are available, wait for clouds to obscure the sun or create your own with a jacket, a commercially available light diffuser, or even yourself. Fill flash (see chapter 4) will warm up your subject and fill in the shadows created by midday's high contrast and top-lighting. A haze filter or, better, a *polarizing filter* will reduce the harsh midday glare and return the richness to colors.

Best light:

♦ **magic hours around sunrise and sunset on sunny days**

♦ **midday on overcast days**

♦ **dramatic light of changing weather**

Worst light:

♦ **harsh overhead lighting (at midday) on sunny days**

Hour before sunset. The light late in the day mirrors that found early in the morning. The light of late afternoon, from an hour or so before the sun sets until it sinks below the horizon, is very similar to that of early morning after sunrise. However, changes occur in reverse order and colors are often bolder and redder because of the atmospheric haze that has developed during the day. It is usually easier to make better photographs during this period because you have plenty of time to find the right composition well before the best light appears.

After sunset. The light from just after the sun sets until darkness prevails is also similar to early morning before sunrise. Once the sun goes down, do not be too quick to pack your gear. Some of the day's best light, such as alpenglow, often occurs a half hour or so after sundown.

Night. At night, the light provided by stars and particularly the moon is great for landscape photography. Except during the full moon, light levels at night are too low for us to see much of anything, but our cameras can record an image if we use very long exposures (see chapter 3). Because we cannot really see night scenes with our eyes, these shots create unique, often eerie, images, never actually seen by anyone. Night exposures are usually very long, sometimes taking many hours; thus, a tripod and *shutter release cable* are required. These long exposures, unfortunately, create a variety of problems covered in chapter 3.

DRAMATIC LIGHT

To make dramatic photographs, look for dramatic light—which, unfortunately, does not happen often and is usually fleeting. But such light can create those unique, high-impact images that all photographers dream of. Because such light comes and goes quickly, anticipation is the key to taking advantage of the drama it creates. Knowing your composition and exposure in advance gives you the time to focus on capturing that drama, rather than on fumbling with gear or running around trying to find the right location. Know what to look for, keep your eyes open, and keep your camera ready.

Dramatic light occurs in situations when the sunlight's character is significantly, and usually briefly, affected by its interaction with the earth's atmosphere. Such light, rich in character, is most often found in two situations, but can occur at other times as well.

The magic hour. During the "magic hours" discussed in the previous section, the rapidly changing light creates evocative images, such as the pre-dawn photograph of Wonderlake in Plate 19 and the photograph of the emperor penguin family in Plate 14 taken with the sun just above the horizon. Haze and moisture in the atmosphere can enhance the effect further, especially at sunset.

Storms. During building or clearing storms, when weather is changing dramatically and rapidly, as in Plate 24, light can take on unusual colors, and the appearance of rainbows, lightning, and crepuscular rays can be an added bonus. Look for patterns of light and dark on the landscape created by shifting clouds, which can create unique images. Combine the magic hour with dramatic weather, such as thunderstorms at sunset, for those once-in-a-lifetime photographs.

Chapter 3

EXPOSURE

Exposure is simply the amount of light allowed to strike the film to create the image that you want. The "correct" exposure means that the subject or most important parts of your photograph look like you wanted them to look. *Overexposure* means these are lighter than you wanted them to be; *underexposure* means that they are darker than you wanted. Note that "correct" exposure is the one that produced the photograph that *you* wanted, which is not necessarily what your camera's light meter thought it should be or what you actually saw. There are many occasions when you will let in more or less light than your meter suggests to get the effect that you want. For example, letting in less light—underexposing—will make billowy white clouds look like a threatening storm. Letting in more light—overexposing—can make a darkening twilight sky look pastel.

Four simple tools are required to make a correctly exposed photograph: film to record the image, an aperture to let light through the lens, a shutter to expose the film to the light coming through the lens, and a way to estimate the intensity of that light. All of these tools are contained inside a small tool box—your camera. This chapter reviews using your camera's aperture and shutter speed to control the amount of light that reaches the film and two ways of measuring light intensity, which determines how much light you have to let in to get the right exposure.

The process of determining exposure is a series of decisions on how to use these tools that starts with you determining what you want your photograph to look like and ends with you pressing the shutter release button. In between, you, with the help of your camera, make decisions on what film speed to use, how to measure the light, how to evaluate that measurement relative to what you want your photograph to look like, and finally what aperture and shutter speed to use. Once you understand the tool set, this decision process becomes much easier, and getting good photographs will no longer be a surprise.

Today's cameras with automatic exposure (AE) can make some or even all of these decisions for you. Sometimes your camera will make correct decisions, but many times it will not. Even if the camera makes technically correct decisions, it will not necessarily make decisions that give you the image that you want. To effectively use automatic exposure, you still need to understand exposure principles and how to apply them. You may let the camera do much of the decision making for you, but at least you will understand what the camera is doing and when to override the automatic settings. But as long as you leave it all up to your camera, you often will not get the unforgettable images that are possible when you fully control the creative process.

USING APERTURE, SHUTTER SPEED, AND FILM SPEED TO CONTROL EXPOSURE

The size of the lens aperture, the length of time the shutter stays open, and film speed, or how sensitive the film is to light, control exposure. Typically, exposure is expressed in terms of an aperture and a shutter speed for a particular film speed. The correct exposure is the combination of aperture and shutter speed, for a given film speed, that gives you the photograph that you want.

Aperture, shutter speed, and film speed are all measured in *stops*. A stop is a relative measure in which each whole unit represents twice the preceding value and half the next higher value. For example, the series "1 ... 2 ... 4 ... 8 ... 16 ... 32" is a range of stops, in which "2" is twice as much as "1" but half as much as "4," which is twice as much as "2" but half as much as "8," and so on. The better you can think in terms of stops—doublings and halvings—the easier managing exposure will be.

Aperture

The aperture is the size of the lens opening through which light travels to the film. The larger the opening, or aperture, the more light gets in. Lenses have a range of openings, called f-stops, with a typical sequence of f/2.8, f/4, f/5.6, f/8, f/11, f/16, and f/22, often with one-third- or one-half-stop increments in between, which are shown on the lens barrel. Each f-stop is an indicator of the size of the aperture: the larger the number in the f-stop, the smaller the aperture.

For example, an aperture of f/2 is a much larger opening, and thus lets in far more light, than an aperture of f/16. This is a doubling and halving scale covering a six-stop range; each successive f-stop lets in half the light of the preceding one, and twice as much as the next one. For example, f/4 lets in half as much light as does f/2.8; f/5.6 lets in half as much light as f/4; f/8 lets in half as much light as f/5.6; and so on.

In addition to determining how much light is let in through the lens to the film, the aperture selection also determines, in part, the depth of field, the zone in front of and behind the subject in which everything is in focus. The area in front of and beyond this zone will appear out of focus.

TIP

When photographing with slide film, try under-exposing by one-third stop to saturate colors.

How big you want the depth of field to be often dictates what aperture you choose when taking a photograph, as discussed in Chapter 1.

As you decrease the size of the aperture by increasing the f-stop number, known as *stopping down*, the depth of field increases. For example, the depth of field increases when you stop down from f/5.6 to f/8, and is the widest at f/22. As you increase the size of the aperture by decreasing the f-stop number, known as *opening up*, depth of field decreases. For example, the depth of field narrows when you open up from f/8 to f/5.6. To illustrate, Plates 3 and 11 have narrow depth of field and were taken with an aperture of f/5.6. Plates 6 and 7 have a wide depth of field and were taken with an aperture of f/22.

Shutter Speed

A shutter is simply a curtain covering the film. When you press the shutter release button, the shutter is opened for the length of time indicated by the shutter speed setting. The shutter speed determines the length of time that light is allowed to strike the film. Shutter speed settings typically range from 8 seconds or slower to 1/4000 second or faster, with speeds of 4 seconds, 2 seconds, 1 second, 1/2 second, 1/4 second, 1/8 second, 1/15 second, 1/30 second, 1/60 second, 1/125 second, 1/250 second, 1/500 second, 1/1000 second, and 1/2000 second in between. Most cameras also have a *"B" or "Bulb" setting* that keeps the shutter open for as long as you hold down the shutter release button, either manually or with a cable extension.

Each shutter speed setting in this sequence represents a stop of light. That is, any given shutter speed lets in twice as much light as the next fastest speed, and half as much light as the next slowest speed. For example, 1/500 second lets in twice as much light as 1/1000 second, but half as much as 1/250 second. Or 1/60 second lets in twice as much light as 1/125 second, and half as much as 1/30 second.

In addition to controlling how long light is allowed to strike the film, shutter speed also determines the effect of motion on your photograph. Slower shutter speeds let in more light and are, therefore, more useful in dimmer light. However, the longer the shutter stays open, the more motion, either by the camera or the subject, will affect the image. Thus, photographs taken at slow shutter speeds, say 1/30 second or slower, may appear blurred if the camera or the subject was moving when you pressed the shutter release button. Faster shutter speeds freeze motion, often producing sharper photographs, but let in less light. How you want, or do not want, motion to impact your photograph usually dictates the shutter speed that you select, as discussed in chapter 1.

Film Speed

Film is a light-sensitive medium upon which an image can be recorded by controlling its exposure to light. *Film speed* is the film's sensitivity to light, or how much light is needed to produce an image, and is indicated by the film's ISO rating, formerly called the ASA rating. The higher the ISO rating or number, the more sensitive the film is to light, which means that less light is required to make the photograph that you want. Films suitable for outdoor photography span a four-stop range from ISO 25 to ISO 400, which translates to a sixteenfold difference in the amount of light needed to record an image. Slower-speed films have lower *ISO numbers*, such as 25 or 50, and require more light. Faster films with higher ISO numbers, such as 400, are more sensitive and require less light to make a photograph of the same scene. In between are film speeds of ISO 64, which is one-third stop faster than ISO 50; ISO 100, which is one stop faster than ISO 50; and ISO 200, which is one stop faster than ISO 100 and two stops faster than ISO 50, but one stop slower than ISO 400.

So why all the choices? Why not just use an ISO 400 film all the time to make the process simpler? Unfortunately, there is a trade-off between film speed and image quality. Faster films tend to be more grainy and less sharp than slower film, but, because they require less light, allow you to shoot at faster shutter speeds. Slower films are less grainy and sharper, but require more light, which often means using slower shutter speeds and a tripod to avoid a blurred image. Most professionals use as slow a film as possible to maximize image quality, resorting to high-speed films such as ISO 400 in only the dimmest light. A medium-speed ISO 100 film often provides the best compromise between speed and sharpness. Yet ISO 200 and 400 films can make excellent photographs. Today's ISO 400 films are comparable to ISO 100 films of the past, which were satisfactory at the time. Experiment with different film speeds to decide what you like.

Reciprocity

The amount of light reaching the film in your camera, sometimes called the exposure value, is determined by two variables, aperture and shutter speed. Both are calibrated in stops, or doublings and halvings, and work together in a reciprocal relationship. That is, to get the same exposure value, a change in one variable can be offset by changing the other variable an equal number of stops in the opposite direction. This relationship, called *reciprocity*, means that a variety of aperture and shutter speed combinations can produce the same exposure value. For example, a setting of 1/8 second and f/22 lets in the same amount of light as 1/30 second and f/11 or 1/125 second and f/5.6.

This relationship is very useful in making exposure choices. Once you have an initial exposure setting, you just work in stops to get the aperture/shutter speed combination that gives you the photograph you want. For example, from an initial exposure, determined by using your camera's light meter, of 1/60 second and f/8, you could increase shutter speed to 1/250 second, which reduces the amount of light let in by two stops. To get the same exposure value, you then must add back two stops of light by opening up the aperture from f/8 to f/4. Or you could stop down from f/8 to f/22, a three-stop decrease. To get the same exposure value, you then add back three stops by decreasing the shutter speed to 1/8 second.

Deciding which combination of aperture and shutter speed to use, then, depends on what you want your photograph to look like. When you are more concerned about the effect of motion, such as when shooting wildlife or action, select the shutter speed that you want first, then select the aperture that provides the correct exposure. If you are using automatic exposure, use Shutter Priority Mode, in which you select the shutter speed and your camera selects the aperture. When depth of field is more important, such as when shooting landscapes, select the aperture you want first, then shutter speed. If you are using automatic exposure, then use Aperture Priority Mode, in which you set the aperture and the camera selects the right shutter speed.

For example, you want to photograph the surrounding peaks during a backcountry camping trip. Using your camera's light meter, you determine that the correct exposure needed to make the image that you want is f/5.6 and 1/1000 second, which is great for freezing action. However, you decide that you need to maximize depth of field to ensure that all the peaks and the foreground are in focus, and that shutter speed does not really matter because the mountains are not going to move. Thus, you stop down, i.e., reduce the size of the aperture, from f/5.6 to f/22, which decreases by four stops the amount of light let in. To let in the same amount of light as you determined that you wanted, you simply decrease the shutter speed by four stops to 1/60 second. This combination lets in the same amount of light but provides the depth of field that you need.

Another example: you want sharp, action-stopping photographs of a group of mountain bikers descending an open canyon on a sunny day in southern Utah. Using *exposure guidelines*, you determine an initial exposure, also called a "base" exposure, of 1/125 second and f/16. However, this shutter speed will not freeze the high-speed motion of the mountain bikers, resulting in a blurred photograph. To stop their motion, you increase the shutter speed to 1/500 second, which lets in two stops less light than 1/125 second. To get a correct exposure, you add two stops of light back by increasing the aperture to f/8. This combination provides the same exposure as the initial combination of 1/125 second and f/16, but gives you the motion-stopping effect that you want.

Reciprocity is also helpful in determining what film speed you should use. For example, you are taking pictures of fast-moving white-water kayakers and you decide that you need a shutter speed of 1/500 second to stop their motion. Unfortunately, it is a bit dreary out, which means you would need an aperture as big as f/2 to get a proper exposure with an ISO 100 speed film, but your lens has a maximum aperture of only f/4, two stops less than needed. How can you let in enough light and still use a fast shutter speed to get the action-stopping shots that you want? Switch to a film that is two stops faster, meaning it requires two stops less light to make the same exposure. The answer: use an ISO 400 speed film.

Unfortunately, if you have a completely automatic camera, like most newer point-and-shoot cameras, you have limited control, if any, over these parameters. The camera determines the speed of the film you load in, and then sets the aperture and shutter speed based on its meter reading. While this is often convenient, you lose a lot of creativity by not being able to control any of these variables. Some automatic point-and-shoots do provide a menu through which you select the type of photograph that you are taking, such as action, portraits, scenics, etc. This menu, in effect, provides you with some control over exposure choices. For example, if you select an action shot, then the camera will pick a shutter speed fast enough to stop the action. Consult your camera's manual for how to do this with your camera.

Most SLR cameras allow you to set all three parameters: aperture, shutter speed, and film speed. This can sometimes be more time consuming, but it provides complete creative control over exposure. Newer SLRs often can also be used completely or partially automatically. Some cameras can automatically set the film speed based on the bar codes printed on the film canister; refer to your camera's manual. In Program Mode, if it has one, the camera sets both shutter speed and aperture, which provides the convenience of a point-and-shoot camera but reduces creative control. In either Shutter Speed or Aperture Priority Mode, you select shutter speed or aperture, respectively, and the camera automatically sets the other variable, which provides more convenience and, in some cases, all the creative control you may need.

MEASURING THE LIGHT INTENSITY
USING EXPOSURE GUIDELINES

A photograph is made with the light that is reflecting from the scene you are photographing back through your lens onto your film. Correct exposure lets in the right amount of this reflected light. To determine a correct exposure, or film speed/aperture combination that will let in sufficient light, you must measure the intensity of the reflected light that will reach your film. There are two ways to do this: exposure guidelines and your camera's light meter.

Exposure guidelines provide inexact but often useful shutter speed/aperture combinations for a given film speed according to the general light conditions, such as bright sun or heavy overcast. Your camera's light meter provides a more precise way to measure light intensity and gives you much more creative control. However, exposure guidelines can be very useful in situations that might fool your light meter, when you do not have time to use the light meter, or when it is not working.

The Sunny f/16 Rule

On a bright sunny day just about anywhere in the world, the proper exposure for most front-lit subjects or scenes is an aperture of f/16 and a shutter speed *nearest* to 1/ISO, where ISO is the speed of the film in your camera. For example, if you are photographing a stand of red-leaved trees with the sun shining directly on them from over your shoulder, using ISO 100 film the correct exposure is f/16 and 1/125 second, which is usually the shutter speed nearest 1/100.

Remembering the reciprocity relationship, you can use any combination of aperture and film speed that lets in the same amount of light let in by the combination of f/16 and 1/ISO. For example, with ISO 100 film, f/22 at 1/60 second, f/11 at 1/250 second, f/8 at 1/500 second, f/5.6 at 1/1000 second, and f/4 at 1/2000 second are all equivalent to f/16 at 1/125 second. Thus, if you want to freeze the motion of your subject, use an aperture of f/8 and a shutter speed of 1/500 second. If you want to maximize depth of field, use f/22 at 1/60 second.

The *Sunny f/16 Rule* applies only to subjects that are medium in *tone*; that is, not too dark and not too light. A light-toned subject, such as a polar bear on snow or a seagull on a sandy beach, reflects more light than a medium-toned subject. Consequently, you have to reduce the amount of light reaching your film by one stop to get a proper exposure. The Sunny f/16 Rule then becomes the Light f/22 Rule—f/22 at 1/ISO or any combination of aperture and shutter speed that lets in the same amount of light. For ISO 100 speed film, that would be f/22 at 1/125 second or any equivalent combination, such as f/11 at 1/500 second.

Dark subjects, such as black bears or very dark rocks, on the other hand, reflect less light. Consequently, you have to increase the amount of light reaching the film by one stop to get a correct exposure. The Sunny f/16 Rule becomes the Dark f/11 Rule—f/11 at 1/ISO or any equivalent combination of aperture and shutter speed. For ISO 100 speed film, that would be f/11 at 1/125 second or any equivalent combination, such as f/16 at 1/60 second.

The Sunny f/16 Rule also applies only to front-lit subjects or scenes with a bright sun shining directly on them. If the subject is sidelit, which means that less light is reflected, then add 1 stop of light to the Sunny f/16 exposure. The correct exposure is then f/11, which lets in one more stop of light than does f/16, at 1/ISO or equivalents. If the subject is backlit, meaning that the sun is behind the subject, then add two stops of light to the Sunny f/16 exposure, The correct exposure is then f/8 at 1/ISO or equivalents.

The Sunny f/16 Rule really works as long as you can see distinct shadows. During the hours of full sunlight, just set the aperture and shutter speed using the Sunny f/16 Rule, remembering to make any necessary adjustments as described above. For example, if you are photographing a camping trip with ISO 400 speed film, try exposure settings of f/16 at 1/500 second. If you are high in the mountains with lots of bright snow and sky filling your viewfinder, try f/22 at 1/500 second. Or if you want a shot of your camping companions with the sun behind them, try f/8 at 1/500 second.

The Sunny f/16 Rule, however, does not work if you cannot see distinct shadows. For example, if the sun is obscured by high clouds or your subject is in a shadow, then you must add more light for a proper exposure. Table 3-1 gives the base exposure settings for a scene that is mostly medium-toned under a variety of light conditions.

Table 3-1. Exposure Guidelines*

Light Conditions	Shadows	ISO 100	ISO 400	Front light	Side light	Back light
Sunny snow or beach	Distinct	1/125	1/500	f/22	f/16	f/11
Bright sun	Distinct	1/125	1/500	f/16	f/11	f/8
Hazy sun	Soft	1/125	1/500	f/11	f/11	f/8
Cloudy bright	None	1/125	1/500	f/8	n/a	n/a
Heavy overcast	None	1/125	1/500	f/5.6	n/a	n/a
Open shade	None	1/125	1/500	f/5.6	n/a	n/a

*Note: These guidelines are for a medium-toned subject well after sunrise and before sunset. Add one stop of light if the subject is dark; subtract one stop of light if the subject is light.

You can use the table for other film speeds. Set the shutter speed nearest 1/ISO and use the same aperture settings dictated by the light conditions. For example, use a shutter speed of 1/60 second for ISO 50 or 64 film, and 1/250 second for ISO 200 film. Use the reciprocity rule to determine other aperture and shutter speed combinations that produce the same exposure but provide the depth of field or motion effect that you want.

Most light meters are not sensitive enough to take readings in very *low light*. Use the exposure guidelines shown in Table 3-2 and *bracket* your shots (discussed later in this chapter). Remember to work in stops, using the reciprocity relationship, if you need to use a shutter speed or aperture different from those given in the table.

Table 3-2. Exposure Guidelines for Low-Light Conditions*

	Film speed	
	ISO 100	ISO 400
Subject	**Shutter speed–Aperture**	
Dawn and dusk	1/8–f/8	1/30–f/11
Sunrise and sunset	1/30–f/8	1/60–f/11
Skyline at dusk	1/15–f/5.6	1/30–f/8
Subjects lit by campfires	1/2–f/4	1/15–f/4
Moonlit landscapes w/o moon	8 min–f/4	2 min–f/4
Moonlit snowscapes w/o moon	4 min–f/4	1 min–f/4
Full moon with telephoto lens	1/125–f/8	1/500–f/8
Quarter moon with telephoto	1/60–f/5.6	1/125–f/8
Aurora borealis	1 min–f/4	1/15–f/4
Well-lit street scene	1/8–f/4	1/30–f/4
Lightning	B–f/5.6	B–f/11

*Note: These are rough estimates; bracket plus/minus one-half to one stop.

Using exposure guidelines is an inexact art. You may want to bracket your exposures by one-third- or one-half-stop increments on either side of the listed exposure to ensure that you get a correct exposure. For example, if the base exposure is 1/125 second and f/8, then shoot another frame halfway between f/5.6 and f/8, and another halfway between f/8 and f/11. If you notice that you are consistently over- or underexposing your photographs, try adding or subtracting one-third or one-half stop to these guidelines. Over time you will develop a feel for these guidelines and what adjustments you have to make under different light conditions and with different-toned subjects to get the exposure that you want.

If your camera has a light meter, use it. However, these guidelines are the only way to measure the light intensity when your light meter is not working, and are also useful in situations when your light meter might be fooled, which happens more often than you might think. These include extreme backlighting conditions, low-light conditions, and when the scenes that you are photographing are filled with a lot of contrast, such as on bright, sunny days.

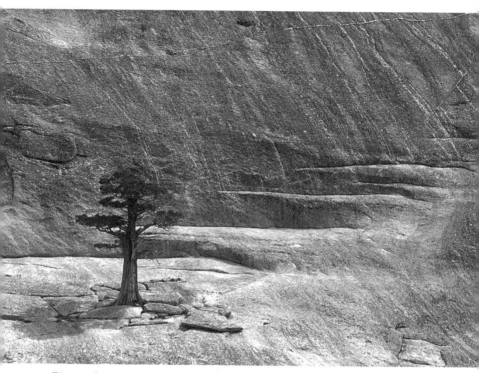

Figure 3-1 Pine Tree, Yosemite National Park, California

These exposure guidelines are also useful when photographing fast action with no time to determine exposure. They work especially well for *print film* because of its wide exposure latitude, which means that you can use a one- to two-stop range of shutter speed/aperture combinations and still get a correctly exposed print. These exposure guidelines do not work well under rapidly changing light conditions, when photographing very small subjects, in early morning or late evening light, or when you want to precisely control exposure.

MEASURING THE LIGHT INTENSITY
USING YOUR CAMERA'S LIGHT METER

Your camera's light meter provides a better way to estimate the intensity of light than exposure guidelines in most situations. Used properly, it provides you with the information you need to make better decisions about exposure settings. However, if you do not use the meter properly or interpret what it is telling you properly, you often will not get the photograph you wanted. Once you understand where to point your camera to take a meter reading, and what that reading is telling you, you can choose the correct exposure setting that will give you what you want.

How the Camera's Light Meter Works

All in-camera light meters, from inexpensive point-and-shoots to the most expensive professional SLRs, work by measuring the light reflected from the scene at which the camera is pointed. This reflected light travels through the lens (known as *TTL*) to the light meter, which, because it measures the light coming through the lens, sees the same light that your film will see after you press the shutter release button. Once your meter has measured this reflected light, you or your camera selects a shutter speed and aperture combination that matches the light level determined by your meter as providing a correct exposure. Consult your owner's manual for how this works with your particular camera. From this base exposure, you then adjust the shutter speed and aperture depending on how you want motion and depth of field to affect your photograph.

Because the meter measures reflected light, the meter reading depends on the overall intensity of the light striking the scene and on the tone of whatever is filling the viewfinder. A meter reading on a bright, sunny day will be very different from a reading on a darker, overcast day. Pointing your camera at something that is very dark, like the fur of a black bear, will result in a very different reading than pointing it at something that is very light, like fresh snow—even when the light intensity is the same.

There are three basic types of meters.

Center-weighted meter. This type of meter assigns more importance to the light in the center of the scene, usually outlined by a large circle in the middle of your viewfinder, than the light from the surrounding area. *Center-weighted metering* works best when you can fill the viewfinder or that circle with the same tone or a simple mix of tones.

Spot meter. A spot meter reads only a very narrow area in the center of the scene and ignores the surrounding area. *Spot metering* is best when you want to take a reading from one object or a particular area within the scene. It provides the most creative control and is widely used by professional photographers.

Matrix or evaluative meter. This type of meter reads the middle area much like a center-weighted meter, but also divides the surrounding area into zones that are evaluated relative to each other and the middle area. *Matrix* or *evaluative metering* is best when light conditions are changing rapidly or the mix of tones is complex and contrast is high, as well as when using fill flash.

Most older cameras have some form of center-weighted metering. Most newer automatic SLR cameras have a center-weighted metering mode and a matrix or evaluative mode, and sometimes even a spot metering mode. Most automatic point-and-shoot cameras have some type of matrix or evaluative meter. Review your camera's manual to understand exactly how your camera's light meter evaluates the scene.

Regardless of the type of meter that you have, whatever is filling the middle of your viewfinder will influence the meter reading the most. If your subject is in the middle of the scene and fills most or all of the viewfinder, it will dominate the reading. If, however, it takes up a small part of the viewfinder and is off center, then the background will dominate the reading. To use your camera's meter reading to get a correct exposure, you have to pay attention to the tone of whatever is filling up the center of your viewfinder.

Light meters should really be called "gray" meters. They are all calibrated to read a medium or average tone that is neither dark nor light, but right in the middle. In a tonal range from white to black, this would be medium gray. In nature, a black bear's fur would be a very dark to black tone, fresh snow would be a very light to white tone, and the gray bark of an oak tree would be a *medium tone*.

However, color does not matter. Any color can be medium- or average-toned, neither very dark nor very light. For example, the blue midnight sky is a very dark tone, the blue sky adjacent to the sun at noon is a very light tone, and the northern blue sky at midmorning is a medium tone. The medium-toned gray tree bark gives about the same meter reading as the medium-toned blue northern sky.

TIP

When using your camera's light meter, remember two things:

- **Whatever fills the middle of your viewfinder will dominate the meter's light reading.**

- **Whatever dominates the light reading will be seen by your light meter as a medium tone. It will try to turn light and dark objects to medium tone.**

Because of this medium-tone calibration, your camera's light meter will not necessarily determine the correct exposure. It only determines the exposure that will make the scene medium-toned, regardless of whether the scene is filled with darker or lighter objects. If the scene you are photographing, or at least the part filling up the center of your viewfinder, is mostly medium-toned, the exposure determined by your

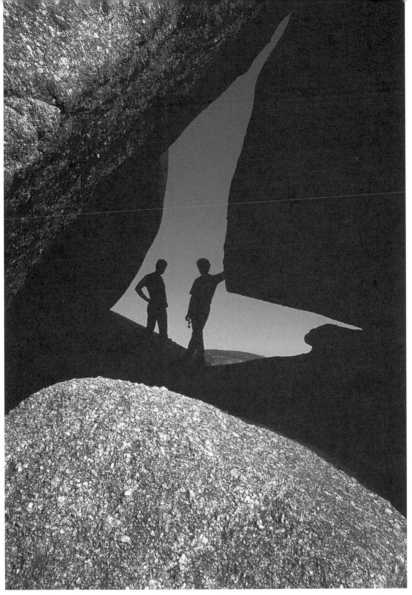

Figure 3-2 Canyonlands, Outback, Australia

light meter will result in a photograph that looks about like the scene it-self. If the scene is mostly very dark, like the wildebeest in Plate 4, your light meter will suggest an exposure that makes it look medium-toned. The resulting photograph will be overexposed; black objects will appear gray, not black. If the scene is mostly very light, like a snow-clad peak in Plate 1, your light meter will again suggest an exposure that makes it look medium-toned. The resulting photograph will be underexposed; the snow will look gray, not white.

Metering on the Subject

There are two ways to take a meter reading, often referred to as *metering*. In the first, you simply point the camera at the subject or most important part of the scene, centering it in your viewfinder, which means that you are "metering the subject." If you have a spot meter, this approach is easy; simply put the small inside circle on the object. For other types of meters, fill as much of the viewfinder as possible with the subject. If your subject does not fill up much of the viewfinder, then your meter will primarily measure the light reflected from the background.

To get a valid meter reading, fill the viewfinder by moving in closer, zooming in, or switching to a longer lens. Once you have a meter reading and have determined exposure, return to your shooting position, zoom back out, or switch back to the original lens. If you do not want the subject or most important part of the image to be in the center of your photograph, move the camera into final position after you have taken a reading and determined exposure. If you are using automatic exposure (AE), lock the exposure setting before repositioning your camera (see your camera's manual).

Once you have metered on your subject, you then must determine the subject's tone. If it is medium-toned, such as the wolf in Plate 2 or the meadow in Plate 8, then you simply set exposure as indicated by the light meter and fire away. If not, then you must adjust the exposure using *exposure compensation*.

Exposure compensation. Exposure compensation is adjusting for your "gray" meter's calibration by adding or subtracting light from the exposure determined by your camera's light meter. Not adjusting for the meter's calibration is a primary cause of bad photographs. You adjust for your camera's "gray" meter calibration by adding light to light and dark to dark. That is, for subjects or scenes lighter than medium tone, like the snowy peak in Plate 1, you add light by using a slower shutter speed, bigger aperture, or both. For subjects or scenes darker than middle tone, like the wildebeest in Plate 4, you subtract light by using a faster shutter speed, smaller aperture, or both.

Table 3-3 provides exposure compensation guidelines for slide film, which can only record a five-stop tonal range. Simply add or subtract stops indicated by the table, depending on the tone of whatever is filling up the center of your viewfinder. Double the adjustments when shooting with print film, which works differently than slide film. For example, instead of adding one stop when photographing a light tone, add two stops.

Table 3-3. Exposure Compensation Guidelines

Tone filling the viewfinder	Number of stops to add or subtract	Shutter speed	f-stop
White	> 2 stops		
Very light	+ 2 stops	1/30 second	f/4
Mostly light	+ 1 1/2 stops		
Light	+ 1 stop	1/60 second	f/5.6
Partly light	+ 1/2 stop		
Medium tone	0 stops	1/125 second	f/8
Partly dark	- 1/2 stop		
Dark	- 1 stop	1/250 second	f/11
Mostly dark	- 1 1/2 stops		
Very dark	- 2 stops	1/500 second	f/16
Black	> 2 stops		

There is, however, one caveat. Few subjects in nature are completely white or black. In the terms of Table 3-3, most white subjects are really "very light" and dark subjects "very dark." Shadows define the detail in truly white subjects, such as a snow-clad peak in Plate 1, while highlights do the same in truly black subjects, such as the backs of the penguins in Plates 14 and 15. If you want this detail, such as the texture of the snow or the swan's individual feathers, to show when using slide film, then do not use more than two stops of exposure compensation. Sometimes one and a half stops is even better. Use two or more stops only when you want the subject to be a completely white or black shape, such as when creating silhouettes.

Exposure compensation can be set by changing the aperture, opening up or stopping down, when you do not want shutter speed to change. For example, if you are metering on the fur of a dark brown bear and the meter indicates a base exposure of f/5.6 at 1/125 second, then subtract light by decreasing the aperture by one stop to f/8.

Alternatively, you can change the shutter speed when you do not want depth of field to change. For example, if you are photographing a snowscape and your meter indicates an exposure of f/22 at 1/60 second, then add two stops of light to ensure that the snow is white in your photograph by reducing the shutter speed to 1/8 second.

You can also adjust both aperture and shutter speed to obtain the appropriate exposure compensation. For example, to subtract one and a half stops of light from a base exposure of f/16 and 1/125 second, you could subtract one stop by increasing the shutter speed to 1/500 second

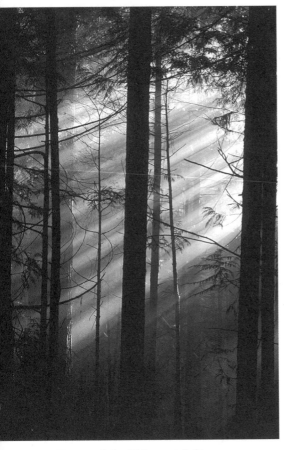

Figure 3-3 Old-growth Forest,
Olympic Peninsula, Washington

and subtract the other half stop by reducing the aperture to halfway between f/16 and f/22.

You can also adjust your camera's ISO setting, increasing it to subtract light and decreasing it to add light, and meter as you normally would. For example, increasing the setting from 100 to 200 effectively subtracts one stop of light, and decreasing it from 100 to 50 adds a stop of light. Remember to reset the ISO setting for the film speed you are using when you do not need exposure compensation.

Use your camera's automatic exposure (AE) compensation capability, if it has one, when you want to make an adjustment for a series of shots. If you use a fully automatic point-and-shoot camera, this may be the only way to use exposure compensation. Again, do not forget to reset the exposure compensation when it is no longer needed. Refer to your camera's manual.

How much exposure compensation is needed is, to some extent, dependent upon your your camera's light meter or on which type of meter you are using, if your camera offers more than one type. These guidelines are most appropriate when using center-weighted and spot meters, especially when only one tone fills the center of the viewfinder. A different exposure compensation may be needed when using matrix or evaluative meters, which compare different areas within the viewfinder to determine exposures. If you have this type of meter in your camera, consult your owner's manual for the manufacturer's recommendations and experiment to see what works.

Metering on a Medium Tone

In the second way to take a meter reading, meter on a medium-toned object or area that is in the same light as the subject or most important part of the scene that you want to photograph. Simply point your camera at that object or area, filling the viewfinder as much as possible, then determine the exposure you want. By reading a medium tone, all the lights and darks will appear as they should, or as you wanted them, and no exposure compensation is needed.

A natural object. Finding a medium tone outdoors is usually easy. Most tree bark, vegetation, animal fur, the northern blue sky about forty-five degrees above the horizon, and rocks are more or less medium tone.

A gray card. A small *gray card* available in photography stores may also be useful, but it is not always convenient to carry or to use on an adventure. To meter, simply hold or place the card in the same light as your subject, point the camera at the card, filling the viewfinder, and determine exposure. However, the light reading from a gray card can change depending on its angle relative to the sun. So follow the directions that come with the card on how to hold it.

A calibrated object. You can also meter on an object that you have calibrated to medium tone by taking meter readings on the object and a gray card in the same light. Just about anything that you frequently take with you on trips, such as jackets, packs, or other items made of fleece, wool, or cotton, will work, as long as it is in the same light as your subject when you take a meter reading. Avoid things made of shiny materials such as coated nylon or metal, as well as things that are very dark or very light.

To determine the object's tone, take meter readings on both it and a gray card in the same light. If it gives the same meter reading as the gray card, then it is medium tone. On trips, meter on the object, making sure that it is in the same light as your subject, and simply use the meter reading as is. No exposure compensation is necessary. If the object is lighter or darker than medium tone, then, when metering outdoors, add or subtract the appropriate exposure compensation. For example, if you are metering on a fleece jacket that you have calibrated to be one-half stop darker than medium tone, then subtract one-half stop from your meter reading to get a correct exposure. If your meter suggests f/5.6 and 1/125 second, set the aperture to halfway between f/5.6 and f/8.

You can also use the palm of your hand. Most people's palms, regardless of race, are approximately one stop lighter than medium tone. Fill your viewfinder with the palm of your hand, holding it in the same light as your subject, and take a meter reading. Because it is one stop lighter, add a stop of light to your meter's reading to get a correct exposure. If your meter suggests f/5.6 and 1/125 second, then add a stop by increasing the aperture to f/4 or decreasing the shutter speed to 1/60 second. Without this adjustment your hand would appear darker than it really is in the resulting photograph. If your palm seems lighter or darker than most, simply compare a meter reading on your palm with one on a gray card in the same light, then apply that amount of exposure compensation.

This substitute-metering approach has several advantages. First, you get to choose the tone that you want to be medium in your photograph. Thus, it provides more creative control. Second, your light measurement is more accurate in high-contrast situations, such as extreme backlighting, that could fool your light meter. Third, it is often easier; you just have to find something that is medium-toned and big or close enough to fill up your viewfinder. It does not even have to be in your photograph. As long as it is in the same light as your subject, you meter, set exposure, then move your camera back into position to get the shot you want. Again, if you are using automatic exposure (AE), lock the exposure setting before repositioning your camera (see your owner's manual).

Metering is now a simple matter of choosing where to point your camera. You do not have to take a meter reading from the exact scene that will become your photograph. In fact, you often will not want to.

For example, say you want to photograph your climbing team on the summit of the peak you have just climbed. You want to show their exuberant faces as well as the surrounding alpine scenery. You frame your shot with a partly cloudy sky in the upper third of the frame, bright

TIP

To create a silhouette, meter on the sky on either side of the subject that you want silhouetted.

snow-clad peaks in the middle third, and your sunlit climbing partners in the bottom third. Your camera's light meter reading will probably be dominated by the bright snow and cloudy sky. Because your meter wants to make everything gray, if you use the meter reading from this scene to set the exposure, the snowy peaks will be gray instead of white and your friends' faces will likely be unrecognizably dark or underexposed.

To get a reading that will give you the results that you want, point your camera at your friends, moving in closer or zooming in if necessary. If they are more or less medium-toned, you simply use the meter's reading. If not, then use exposure compensation for the differences in tone by adding or subtracting light. Once you have your reading and exposure set, reposition the camera to take the shot you want. Alternatively, you can meter on some nearby gray rocks that are in the same light as your companions, set your exposure, and reposition your camera for the shot.

Again, if you are using automatic exposure, be sure to press the AE lock before repositioning your camera.

Finding a Medium Tone

To take useful light readings, both you and your camera's light meter must be able to read a medium tone as a medium tone. If your pictures are consistently under- or overexposed, then one or the other is not properly calibrated.

Learning to read a medium tone. To calibrate yourself, you must learn to recognize a medium tone when you see one, and, when there is no middle tone, how much darker or lighter than medium a particular tone is. Several exercises can help you do this.

First, take meter readings off of a gray card or some other medium-toned object, such as the blue northern sky about forty-five degrees above the horizon any time between midmorning and midafternoon. Compare them with readings from various tones that are in the same light as the gray card or, if using the northern sky, fully lit by the sun.

Second, shoot a series of pictures in which you meter what you think is a medium tone. Take one photograph at the exposure suggested by your light meter, then one at one-half stop under that exposure, then one stop under, one-half stop over, and one stop over. Then, after you have processed the film, compare the five photographs to see if what you thought was medium-toned actually was. You can repeat this exercise for light and dark tones to get a feel for how far under and over they are from medium tone.

Finally, take notes in the field on what you metered when you took a particular photograph and the exposure settings, which are meaningless unless you know how you metered the scene. Eventually you will develop a good feel for what is a medium tone.

When photographing outdoors, look for a dark to very dark tone in the scene you are shooting that is in the same light as your subject. Then find a light to very light tone in the scene (also in the same light as your subject). These now represent the endpoints of a tonal scale for that scene. Finally, look for a tone that appears to be about halfway between the two end tones and meter on it. For example, in Plate 15, the chests of the penguins are the lightest tone, their backs are the darkest, and the chick's chest is in between the two. This is essentially how most matrix or evaluative light meters work. They compare the tones of different zones or segments in the scene that fills the viewfinder. If you have a spot meter, you can easily compare the tones yourself, which enables you to exercise greater creative control.

Calibrating your camera's light meter. Camera light meters are often inaccurate even though they are calibrated by the manufacturer to read a medium tone. But then, so was your car's gas gauge. When it shows "empty," you know from experience that you still have, for example, an eighth of a tank left. So you make that mental adjustment and keep on driving. Likewise, you need to know how far off of medium tone your light meter reads so you can make any adjustment needed for a correct exposure, especially when using slide film. Small deviations from a medium-tone calibration can have a big impact on slides but a relatively small impact on print film because the proper tones can be restored when printing the negative.

To calibrate your camera's meter, use the Sunny f/16 Rule. On a bright sunny summer morning, position a gray card, or any other medium-toned object, directly in the sunlight. With the sun shining over your shoulder onto the gray card, point your camera at the card, filling the viewfinder. If your camera is loaded with film, set your shutter speed to the setting nearest to 1/ISO. For example, with ISO 50 film, set the shutter speed to 1/60 second, or with 1SO 100, to 1/125 second. If your camera is not loaded with film, set your film speed to ISO 64 and the shutter speed to 1/60 second.

Now, set the aperture to f/16. If your camera's meter indicates that this is the correct exposure, then your meter is properly calibrated. If not, then adjust your film speed (ISO) until a correct exposure is indicated. Your meter is off by the number of stops you had to adjust the film speed to get a correct exposure at an aperture of f/16.

To compensate, simply make the same adjustment whenever you load your camera with film. For example, with ISO 64 film, suppose you reduced the film speed to ISO 50 to get a correct exposure at f/16. That means your meter is off by one-third stop. You should reduce the film speed by one-third stop whenever you take pictures. For ISO 50 film, set the film speed to ISO 40; for ISO 64 film, set it to ISO 50; for ISO 100, set

METERING

Metering your subject:

♦ **Fill viewfinder with subject or most important part of the scene**

♦ **What tone is filling the middle of the viewfinder?**

▪ *If medium,* **use your light meter's exposure settings**

▪ *If light,* **add light by decreasing shutter speed or increasing aperture**

▪ *If dark,* **subtract light by increasing shutter speed or decreasing aperture**

Metering a middle tone:

♦ **Fill viewfinder with a medium tone in the same light as your subject**

♦ **Use your light meter's exposure settings**

it to ISO 80; and so on. For an even more precise calibration, repeat the exercise with all the different films that you use, because your camera may need to be adjusted differently for each one.

Fooling Your Camera's Light Meter

Your camera's light meter is easily fooled in some situations. For example, sunny, high-contrast scenes filled with well-lit areas—called highlights—and dark shadows often provide meter readings that do not produce the photograph that you wanted. Depending on how you took your meter readings, highlights can become burnt-out white areas and dark shadows can become dense black areas in your photograph. When photographing such scenes, keep the limitations of your film in mind when metering and determining exposure. Film cannot record the full range of light found in such high-contrast scenes.

As a general guideline, when shooting with slide film, meter on an object or area in the well-lit part of the scene, a technique referred to as "metering the highlights." This eliminates any bright white spots or areas in your photograph that will detract from your composition and lets the shadows turn very dark to black. With print film, do the opposite; meter the shadows. As long as you do not burn out the highlights completely, the printing process usually produces a photograph that looks about right, although you may have to work with the printer to get exactly what you want.

Other situations may also fool your camera's light meter. Backlighting, especially when the subject is dark against a much brighter background, can skew the meter reading even if the subject is right in the middle of the viewfinder. To compensate, add two or more stops of light or meter only your subject by moving in close, zooming in, or using a spot meter, if your camera has one.

A well-lit subject against a very dark background may also fool the meter, especially if the subject is very light-toned. The dark background may dominate the meter reading. To compensate, subtract one to two stops of light or move in close to meter. If your camera has a matrix or evaluative metering mode, use it in these types of situations.

Fog, mist, and precipitation can also play tricks on your meter, which may read the light reflecting from the fog rather than the subject. To compensate, add a stop to your exposure determination, depending on how bright the fog is. Or move in close to meter or spot meter an object not covered by the fog.

Readings from matrix or segmented evaluative meters may also be skewed when a small portion of the viewfinder is very bright or very dark relative to the rest of the scene. For example, a cloudy bright sky filling the upper corner of the viewfinder when you are photographing a rock climber on dark rock may skew the meter reading enough to underexpose the climber. To get a correct reading, point the camera at the subject, eliminating the sky from the viewfinder. Then move the camera back into position to get the shot you want.

EXPOSURE IN LOW LIGHT

Early morning, twilight, overcast skies, deep shadows, forest interiors, and other low-light situations often provide a quality of light that produces great images. However, the relatively low light levels during these periods create problems that complicate the exposure puzzle. Shutter speeds may have to be too slow to freeze the action of a moving subject or even handhold your camera. In fact, shutter speeds may be so slow that normal exposure rules no longer apply, especially when using small apertures to maximize depth of field. In addition, light meters may not be sensitive enough to measure such low levels of reflective light. Thus, determining exposure requires you to play tricks with your light meter or to use exposure guidelines.

Slow Shutter Speeds

At lower light levels, you may have to use shutter speeds too slow to stop the movement of your subject or your camera at a given aperture. This problem can frequently be encountered when using slower but sharper films. Even in relatively bright conditions such as a cloudy bright day or in the shadows on a sunny day, there is just not enough light to use fast shutter speeds with such slow films. If subject motion is not a problem but the required shutter speed is too slow to effectively handhold the camera, then use some form of camera support, such as a tripod, and a cable release.

Really slow shutter speeds. Shutter speeds of 1 second or more, often required before sunrise and after sunset, result in reciprocity failure, meaning that normal exposure rules no longer apply. Determining exposure by normal means results in underexposed images. To counteract reciprocity failure, add one-half to one extra stop of light to get a correct exposure. As a general rule, add one-half stop for 4- to 8-second exposures and one stop for exposures longer than 8 seconds. For more exact adjustments, follow the film manufacturers' guidelines on reciprocity failure, which are usually available with the film or at camera stores. For shutter speeds of many minutes or hours, do not worry about compensating for reciprocity failure.

In addition to reciprocity failure, many films also show a subtle color shift, especially with very long shutter speeds of many minutes or hours. Film manufacturers suggest color-correcting filters to counteract this shift. Consult their technical data for which filter to use. However, for most outdoor photography, do not worry about using such filters. In fact, these color shifts can create some interesting effects.

Increasing shutter speed. If, however, you want to stop subject motion, then you have to shoot at a faster shutter speed. According to the reciprocity relationship, the only way to do that when there is not enough light is to reduce the amount of light required by the film to make the image that you want. That is, you have to shoot at a faster film speed or higher ISO number. There are two ways to do this.

First, you can switch to a faster film. If an ISO 50 film is not fast enough, switch to an ISO 100 film, which allows you to double your shutter speed. If that is not enough, try ISO 400, which is three stops faster than an ISO 50 film. However, faster films are not as sharp as slower films, so you may not want to use them, or you may not have any faster film with you.

Second, rather than switching to a faster film, you can "push" the film you have. Set the film speed on your camera to the next highest whole-ISO number, which buys you an extra stop of light, or the next highest shutter speed. Then, when you have your film processed, specify a "one-stop" push. The lab will then process the film as if it were a one-stop-faster film. For example, to push ISO 100 film one stop, set the ISO to 200 on your camera and specify a one-stop push at the lab that will process it, and it will be processed as if it were ISO 200. Most slide films can be pushed one stop with excellent results. Some can even be pushed two stops; experiment to see what works. Pushing your film one to two stops buys you an extra shutter speed setting or two, but may result in some increase in contrast and graininess, although usually less than that exhibited by a faster film.

Metering in Low-Light Situations

When you want to maximize depth of field, you determine exposure by first selecting a small aperture, such as f/16 or f/22, then taking a meter reading to determine what shutter speed to select for a correct exposure. However, in low-light situations, the required shutter speed may be longer than the slowest speed available on your camera, which means your meter cannot measure such a low level of light.

To determine shutter speed, use the reciprocity relationship. First, open up to the largest aperture (f/2.8), take a meter reading, and adjust your shutter speed to get a correct exposure. Next, stop back down to the desired aperture, counting the number of stops between f/2.8 and the final aperture. Then decrease the shutter speed by that number of stops, adding additional stops as needed for reciprocity failure.

For example, at an aperture of f/2.8, you meter and determine that a shutter speed of 1 second provides a correct exposure. You then stop down to f/22, subtracting six stops of light. To end up with a correct exposure, you must add back six stops by using a shutter speed of 60 seconds. Because of reciprocity failure, you must also add another stop of light, making the appropriate shutter speed 2 minutes. If the slowest speed on your camera is less than that, set the shutter speed to "B" and use your watch to measure 2 minutes.

If you still cannot determine exposure, use the same method, but meter on something lighter than a medium tone. For example, to get the correct shutter speed, meter on your hand and add one stop, or meter on a white T-shirt and add two stops, again adding any additional stops as needed to counteract reciprocity failure. If that still does not work, extend the reciprocity relationship by adjusting the ISO rating to a higher number, take a meter reading, reset to the correct ISO, and reduce the shutter speed by the number of stops between the ISO rating at which you metered and the correct ISO, adding any additional stops to counteract reciprocity failure. If you use this approach, be sure to reset the ISO rating correctly.

MULTIPLE EXPOSURES

Shooting multiple images on the same frame of film can make for some interesting effects, such as putting a moon into a scene or creating a surrealistic collage. When shooting multiple-exposure images in which the images will not overlap but one image will overlay a black area on the preceding image, then expose each image normally. For example, when placing a full moon from a dark sky above a landscape with a black sky, shoot the moon, positioned high in the frame, at 1/125 second at f/8 for ISO 100 film. The moon will be properly exposed and the sky below the moon, where the landscape will be in the second image, will be black because there was insufficient light to expose the film. Then reposition the camera with the landscape at the bottom of the frame with plenty of black sky above. Determine the exposure for the landscape, and shoot the second image.

However, when shooting multiple-exposure images, each shot must receive less exposure than it would if shot as a single image. The more images, the more the exposure must be reduced for each individual shot, as shown in Table 3-4. To get a correct exposure, first determine exposure for the scene as you normally would. Then decrease that exposure by the number of stops indicated in the table for the number of images that you plan to shoot on the same frame.

Table 3-4. Exposure Compensation for Multiple Exposures

Number of Images	Number of stops	ISO change
1	0	100
2	- 1	200
3	- 1 1/2	320
4	- 2	400
5	- 2 1/4	500
6	- 2 1/2	640
7	- 2 3/4	n/a
8	- 3	800

For example, if the exposure to shoot a single image of a flower field is 1/125 second at f/8 with ISO 100 film, then to shoot four images on the same frame, the correct exposure would be two stops less, or 1/60 second at f/5.6.

Alternatively, you can multiply the ISO number of the film in your camera by the number of exposures you plan to take. Adjust the ISO on your camera to the setting on your camera closest to this number (see Table 3-4), determine exposure as you normally would in either manual or automatic mode, and fire away. Be sure to reset to the correct ISO when you are done. For example, to shoot four exposures on the same frame with ISO 100 film, set the ISO on your camera to 400 (four times 100), determine exposure, and shoot.

WHEN TO BRACKET

Bracketing, or taking a series of shots under and over the initial exposure you determined to be correct, is often pooh-poohed by more technical-minded photographers, overused by many less skilled snapshooters, and highly recommended by film manufacturers. While bracketing should not replace a working knowledge of determining and controlling exposure, it can be very useful in two situations, especially when using slide film. With print film, bracketing is usually unnecessary because the negative can be printed in several ways as if it were shot at different exposures.

For a golden opportunity. When you have the shot of a lifetime and you are not quite sure what the best exposure should be, bracket. If you have spent lots of time, effort, or money to photograph a glorious sunrise in a faraway place, bracketing is cheap insurance that you will indeed have the best image possible when you get back home. If you encounter a Yeti in the Himalayas, or any other truly remarkable subject, bracket. A bad shot of a Yeti will be valuable; a great shot will be priceless. Film is cheap compared to the cost of not getting the most out of opportunities like these. But do not overdo it; save some film for the next golden opportunity.

For different effects. When you want to create multiple images of a scene with different effects or looks, bracket. In many situations, different exposures of the same scene can result in images with very different moods or messages. For example, take a series of sunset or sunrise shots using a range of exposures, from two stops under to two stops over. Then compare the results to see the different effects. Overexposures with softer, pastel colors are often more restful and cheerful, while underexposures with darker, bolder colors are often more dramatic or somber. With backlit subjects, an underexposure relative to your meter reading would produce a silhouette, while an overexposure would produce a normal-looking subject against a bright background. Both photographs would acceptably represent the same subject, but would produce quite different reactions from viewers.

However, there are many other situations in which the correct exposure works, but even one-third of a stop under or over looks terrible. For example, people, animals, plants, or other familiar objects will look normal, as people would expect them to look, in photographs taken with the correct exposure. However, photographs of subjects often will not look natural if they are much darker or lighter than expected. In these cases, determine correct exposure and save the extra film for more correctly exposed shots of the same scene but from different points of view.

Chapter 4

WORKING WITH YOUR CAMERA GEAR

Careful use of your camera gear in the field is critical to making great photographs. Even the best composition taken with a correct exposure will make a lousy picture if you do not handle your gear properly. On the other hand, using your gear to its best advantage often makes the difference between a mediocre photograph and an excellent one. Pleasing composition, the right light, appropriate exposure, and careful field technique add up to excellent photography. This chapter covers a variety of techniques, tips, and guidelines for working with your equipment to get the sharpest, highest-quality pictures possible, ones that you can enlarge and display proudly.

TAKING YOUR CAMERA ALONG

Carrying camera gear, yet having easy access to it while you are active outdoors, is one of the tougher challenges of adventure photography, especially if you are carrying other outdoor or travel gear like food, water, clothing, and rainwear. If you keep your camera buried in your pack, it is easy to carry and well protected—but it is inaccessible. You will only take pictures when you stop for a rest, and you will often be too tired to bother with that. Carrying the camera slung around your neck as you would in town leaves it unprotected and more of a nuisance. Shoulder bags, which are great for shooting during car trips and relatively sedentary activities, are cumbersome and uncomfortable to carry over long distances, especially while you are active.

Land travel. For comfort, protection, and accessibility, carry your camera in a padded case, with an extra lens or two, if needed, in a separate lens case, and accessories and extra film in yet another pouch—all loaded onto your backpack's hip belt. Other outdoor gear and extra camera equipment can be stowed inside your backpack. When you are skiing, biking, or otherwise very active, carry the camera case on your chest with a harness that provides the best compromise between accessibility, protection, and stability. Alternatively, carry the essentials—camera, lenses, film, and accessories—in a padded photo fanny pack, which can be worn in front when carrying your backpack or in back when skiing, biking, etc. For larger amounts of camera gear, use a camera or photo backpack that is big enough to have room left over for other outdoor gear.

Water travel. Cameras can also be easily protected yet remain accessible even on water-based adventures. Padded dry bags keep cameras at hand and dry if used properly. Waterproof hard cases with o-rings are ideal for carrying larger amounts of camera gear. These can be lashed to your boat while traveling. To shoot while you are actually on the water, use a camera designed for underwater use or your own camera inside a waterproof housing, which is available in a soft, more flexible version and a hard, more protective version. Waterproof cameras and housings can often be rented, especially at more popular aquatic destinations.

Air travel. Traveling by air with camera gear presents additional problems, especially when traveling between countries. Whenever possible, hand carry your camera gear in a well-padded but nondescript pack or case. To minimize the chances of theft, avoid bags that are obviously camera bags and carry your gear in front of you where you can keep an eye on it. If you must check camera gear through as baggage, bury it deep inside a nondescript bag surrounded by clothing. Use foam or inflatable sleeping pads for extra protection and wrap duct tape around the bag.

ELIMINATING CAMERA MOVEMENT

Camera movement while shooting is one of the primary causes of blurred pictures. Just holding the camera in your hand can cause significant movement no matter how still you try to be. The act of pressing the shutter release button can rotate the camera enough to blur your pictures, especially if the camera is not well supported. Even a stiff breeze can easily move your camera enough to blur your pictures, especially if you are using a telephoto lens. Some simple techniques, a good camera support, and a few key accessories can minimize these problems and improve your photographs.

Handholding Your Camera

To minimize camera movement while shooting, hold the camera body with your right hand with the index finger positioned to press the shutter release button. Cradle the bottom of the camera and lens in the palm of your left hand, using your fingers to turn the focusing and aperture rings. If shooting vertically, swing your right hand up with your left hand underneath, and brace your left elbow against your stomach. When you take the picture, hold your elbows firmly against the sides of your body and gently press or squeeze the shutter release button with the index finger of your right hand. If you are breathing heavily from exertion or excitement, wait until your breathing and heart rates have returned to normal before taking pictures, or increase your shutter speed as much as possible.

When handholding your camera, use the fastest shutter speed possible. As a guideline, use the shutter speed closest to the focal length of the lens being used or faster. For example, when shooting with a 50mm lens, the minimum shutter speed should be 1/60 second. For a 105mm lens, the minimum should be 1/125 second. The longer the lens, the faster the shutter speed must be to get a sharp photograph, which, in practice, limits the lens length you can handhold to about 200mm.

At least double that minimum shutter speed when shooting while walking, breathing heavily from exertion, or otherwise moving while photographing. The minimum shutter speed for that 50mm lens becomes 1/125 second, or faster, the faster you are moving. Conversely, you can cut the recommended shutter speed in half, allowing you to shoot in lower light, by bracing yourself against a solid object like a tree or resting your elbows on a flat surface or solid object. The minimum shutter speed for that 50mm lens would then be 1/30 second. When there is not enough light to shoot at the minimum shutter speed, open up the aperture, switch to faster film, or use some sort of camera support.

Camera Supports

Using some form of camera support whenever possible will eliminate camera movement, resulting in sharper pictures and allowing you to shoot at much lower shutter speeds. No matter how still you think you can hold your camera, a solid support will always do a better job. Without a camera support, the lowest shutter speed that will produce acceptably sharp images is 1/60 second or 1/125 second for most outdoor

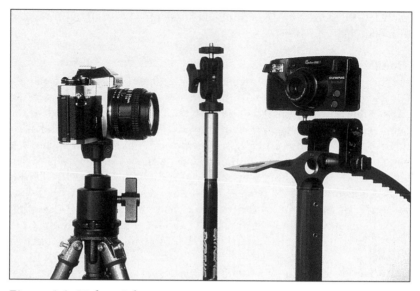

Figure 4-1 Lightweight camera supports

photographers. However, most cameras are capable of shooting at much slower speeds, and thus in much lower light. There are many situations, such as early morning, overcast days, or deep inside a forest, in which there is just not enough light, even with higher-speed film like ISO 400, to handhold a camera. Thus, without camera support you will inevitably miss a lot of excellent photo opportunities, especially because many of them occur when the light is low. Camera supports that work well for outdoor and adventure photography are shown in Figure 4-1.

Tripods. A sturdy tripod with a secure tripod head, like the one shown in Figure 4-1, is the best means of supporting your camera while shooting or waiting for the right moment to shoot. A tripod does add weight and can be a nuisance to carry, but the benefits far exceed the extra effort. Using a tripod will not only result in sharper pictures, but will also allow you to take the time to do things right and eliminate the fatigue of handholding what can become a tiresome weight. Without a tripod, it is impossible to get sharp pictures using slower shutter speeds or longer lenses, and difficult to precisely focus. Once you get used to using one in the field, you will not want to shoot without it.

In general, the heavier the tripod is, the better it will support the camera. Use the heaviest tripod and head that you are willing to carry. For field work, a medium-weight (five to eight pounds) tripod and a solid ball head will support heavier cameras and lenses even in the toughest of conditions. The tripod's legs should be long enough to put the camera at eye level, should open completely, which allows you to get your camera near the ground for close-up shots, and should open independently of each other, which allows you to use the tripod on uneven terrain. The ball head should be removable, be well machined with a smooth action even when loaded, and have a quick release.

When it is not possible to carry such a combination, a relatively lightweight "backpacking" tripod can still be more than adequate if used properly. However, many such tripods are poorly constructed of cheap materials, do not hold up well in the field, and are a real pain to work with because they are top heavy and the head movement is typically very limited. Well-made tripods in the two- to three-pound range with round, extruded legs and a lightweight ball head, as shown in Figure 4-1, are ideal for more adventurous trips when you cannot carry something more substantial. To save weight yet have sufficient stability, get a tripod with shorter but still solid legs, rather than spindly but full-length legs. These lighter-weight models will support the typical camera with shorter lenses or longer but slower lenses like a 75mm–300mm f/4–f/5.6. They are also ideal for compact point-and-shoot cameras. However, they are not adequate for serious macro or wildlife photography.

When using a lighter-weight tripod, avoid extending the legs completely or extending the center post. You may have to sit, kneel, or bend awkwardly, but the tripod will be far more stable. If you do have to extend such a tripod completely, you can add stability by adding weight. Simply hang your pack or a stuff sack filled with rocks between the tripod's legs. If possible, have the stuff sack just touching the ground to in effect add a fourth leg and even more stability. You can save weight by removing the tripod's center post and mounting the head directly onto the legs, or replacing it with a shorter one.

Whatever tripod you have, insulate the legs either with commercially available tripod leg wraps or with plumbing-pipe insulation wrapped in duct tape, both of which are available at the hardware store. The insulation will provide padding when carrying the tripod over your shoulder and protect your hands from cold metal when shooting in cooler temperatures. When using the tripod on snow, put the feet on top of pieces of closed-cell foam pad, plastic plates, or Frisbees to prevent the legs from sinking into the snow.

Using a tripod to shoot moving subjects with a telephoto lens allows you to shoot at quite slow shutter speeds when the subject stops moving. Set the tension on the ball head loosely enough so you can move the camera with the action, but tightly enough so that the camera is well supported when you press the shutter release button. Then you can track the subject's motion and be ready to shoot when it stops. Make sure that your camera is very securely attached to the tripod head, especially if the lens is attached rather than the camera body. Moving the camera around can loosen the connection or, worse, stress and potentially damage the threads in the tripod mount as well as the lens mount.

"Table-top" or "pocket-sized" tripods are lighter-weight but less flexible alternatives to a full-sized tripod. These mini-tripods are ideal for climbing, adventure travel, and other types of photography where weight and bulk are seriously limited. You can almost always find a rock, countertop, or other solid surface to put them on. If not, lie on the ground, a vantage point that provides an unusual perspective and is often the best for close-up shots. These are fine for compact point-and-shoots and lightweight SLRs with shorter lenses.

Beanbags. Beanbags can also turn just about any solid object, such as a rock, fence post, or even your car door, into a camera support. While the support on which you rest the beanbag could hold the camera alone, the beanbag allows you to easily position the camera to get the shot you want and cradles the lens, providing additional support. Without the beanbag, you would have to place sticks or rocks under your lens to position the camera, which is time consuming and reduces stability.

Several commercial models of beanbags are available, both with and without "beans." These can be easily carried unfilled in your pack or camera bag; then, when needed, simply fill loosely with dirt or pebbles to create an instant camera support. In a pinch, your pack, a stuff sack loosely filled with clothing, your jacket, or even coiled climbing ropes make adequate "beanbags." Beanbags can support just about any camera and even longer, heavier lenses.

Clamps. As shown in Figure 4-1, there are a variety of other camera supports useful in outdoor and travel photography when shooting with relatively short lenses and lighter-weight cameras. A clamp with a small ball head that also serves as a table-top tripod is a flexible accessory. The clamp turns tree limbs, signposts, ice axes, pack frames, or just about anything else up to two to three inches wide, into a camera support.

Camera mounts. A variety of ski poles and walking sticks can be fitted with an optional camera mount. Look for ones that can accept or include a small ball head.

Monopods. Monopods, quicker but less stable than their three-legged cousins, are great for action photography and can be used with longer lenses.

Shutter Release Cable

In addition to some form of camera support, use a shutter release cable to eliminate any camera movement that you might cause when pressing the shutter release button—especially when shooting at slower shutter speeds or with your camera precariously perched on a rock or log. Even when your camera is mounted onto a tripod, pressing the shutter release button can rotate the camera, which can blur your photograph. Consult your camera's manual for details on how to use a cable with your camera.

If you do not have a shutter release cable or your camera cannot accept one, then use your camera's self-timer. Either way, by not pressing the shutter release button with your finger, your own heavy hand will not blur your photographs.

WORKING WITH LENSES

For some considerations in choosing lenses, refer to Techniques to Enhance Composition, chapter 1. To care for your lenses, keep the glass at both ends of your lenses as clean as possible. A large blower is the best way to remove dust and other particles that lenses seem to attract like a magnet. If the blower does not work, use a soft, anti-static brush to gently brush away dirt. But do not get too compulsive; a few dust particles will not affect your photographs. For smudges, gently wipe the glass surface with a very fine lens cleaning cloth, using a gentle, circular motion. Always start in the center and move outward to the edges. If the weather is not too cold and damp, it may help to add moisture by breathing on the lens first. Avoid cheap lens tissue; an ultra-fine cleaning cloth cleans far better and leaves no lint. For those really stubborn stains, use a cotton swab or a lens tissue with a drop of lens cleaning solution or alcohol, again gently wiping in a circular motion. However, use cleaning solution sparingly; it may leave a hard-to-remove film on your lens.

Lens *flare*, caused by light reflecting off the glass inside your lens, for example when the sun shines directly on the front of the lens, can ruin an otherwise excellent image. Zoom lenses, filters, very slow shutter speeds, shooting directly at a light

TIP
To avoid flare, shade the front of your lens when shooting into the sun.

source, and scenes with backlight or lots of reflected light can make lens flare even worse. To minimize flare, use the lens hood made for your lens whenever possible. Be careful with generic, one-size-fits-all lens hoods, which may obscure the corners of your photograph, called *vignetting*. When you cannot use the lens hood, shade the front of the lens with your hand or hat or shoot from a shady spot. As a final step, remove any filters that may be on your lens unless you absolutely need the filter's effect.

Focusing

Focusing your lenses appropriately is critical to producing quality images. However, a variety of factors can complicate this apparently obvious and simple dictum.

Unless a photograph is an obvious abstraction, people expect the subject of a picture, or at least key parts of the subject such as an animal's eyes, to be in focus. So make sure that the subject or most important parts of your image are in focus. This is another reason to know exactly what your photograph's subject is, because you cannot focus properly if you do not know what to focus on.

Autofocus. You must be able to see your subject clearly. It is difficult to focus on what you cannot see well even if you are focusing in the right place. Autofocus can be helpful, especially in low light, because your camera's autofocusing capabilities are often better than your own. Consult your camera's manual for details on how to use autofocus in your camera.

Focusing screen. If your camera has a split-center prism screen that can be interchanged, replace it with a bright matte *focusing screen* with an architectural grid, which can be used as a compositional aid and helps keeps your image parallel to the horizon.

Focus indicator. When focusing manually, use the focus indicator, if your camera has one, to augment your own eyesight; consult your camera's manual. At low light levels, shining a flashlight on your subject may help you manually focus. A headlamp allows you to look through the viewfinder and illuminate your subject simultaneously.

Finally, keep the path through which light travels between your eye and the subject as clean as possible. Wipe the camera's eyepiece clean with a soft cloth and use a soft brush or blower on the reflex mirror and the focusing screen above the mirror. Do not use lens cleaner or alcohol inside the camera, but use a blower to remove dirt while you are in there. Be sure to remove dark glasses or ski goggles while focusing.

If it is cold out, be sure to turn your head to the side when looking through the viewfinder; otherwise, your breath will fog the eyepiece.

Depth of Field

Although focusing on the right spot is critical, managing depth of field—the distance in front of and behind that spot within which the image is still in focus—is also very important. This can be tricky because you see a scene differently than does your camera. Your eyes essentially have unlimited depth of field, so you tend to see everything in focus unless you are looking at something that is very close to you. However, lenses have a widely ranging depth of field, depending on the distance between the camera and the subject, the size of the aperture, and the lens's focal length. For example, if the lens's aperture is small, then depth of field will be quite deep, which means that the camera sees most of the scene in focus. However, if the lens's aperture is large, the depth of field will be shallow, meaning that the camera sees only a very narrow part of the scene in focus.

In general, you should adjust the aperture to make the depth of field just large enough to put your subject completely in focus. A smaller aperture increases depth of field, which ensures that your subject is entirely in focus but may result in a more distracting background. A larger aperture reduces depth of field, resulting in parts of the subject being out of focus. If the depth of field is narrower than the subject even at the smallest aperture, such as when shooting close-ups or with a long telephoto lens, then make sure that the part of the subject closest to you is in focus.

In general, depth of field extends further beyond the point at which the lens is focused than in front of that point. When the lens is focused within a few feet of the camera, these distances are essentially the same. When focused further away, depth

> **TIP**
>
> **Focus just in front of the most important part of the scene or subject.**

of field can extend beyond the in-focus point out to infinity. Thus, for most scenes or subjects, focus on a spot one-quarter to one-third of the way into the scene, or the important part of the scene, that you are photographing. When shooting a subject that is very close to you or when depth of field is very narrow, such as when using large apertures, focus on the part of the subject that you most want to be in focus in your photograph.

Depth-of-field preview button. To manage the depth of field to your best advantage, use your depth-of-field preview button or the depth-of-field scale on your lens. When you look through your viewfinder, your lens is wide open, which lets in more light and makes focusing and composition easier. However, what you see is not what you are going to get in your photograph unless you are actually using the biggest aperture. You cannot see the true depth of field. The preview button reduces the size of the lens opening to the selected aperture, allowing you to see exactly what within the scene you are photographing is in focus. Use the preview button to try a variety of apertures until you find the depth of field that you like. However, at very small apertures, when the depth of field is the widest, the viewfinder will become quite dark when you push the preview button. When this happens, shield your eye and the eyepiece with your hands and wait for your pupil to adjust to the low light level.

Depth-of-field scale. If your camera does not have a depth-of-field preview button, then use the depth-of-field scale on your lens or the *hyperfocal distance* table included in this section. To use the depth-of-field scale, first select an aperture and focus on your subject. Then look at the scale on your lens barrel. As shown in Figure 4-2, the distance index line indicates the distance to the subject or point of focus. On either side of the index line are a series of lines, each with one end pointing to the distance scale and the other end pointing to an aperture. The depth of field is the distance that appears on the distance scale between the pair of lines that point to the aperture to which your lens is set. For example, in Figure 4-2, the lens is focused to 10 feet and the aperture is set to f/11. The depth-of-field scale indicates that everything between about 7 and 20 feet will be in focus. If the same lens was focused to 20 feet and the aperture set to f/16, then the depth of field would extend

Figure 4-2 Depth-of-field set at f/11

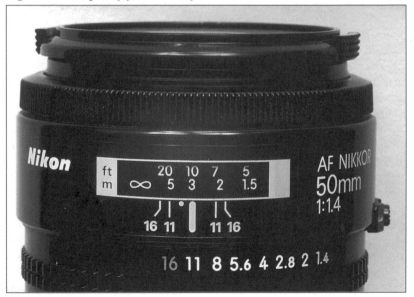

from about 10 feet out to infinity. Consult your lens's manual for details on using this scale for your lens.

Hyperfocal distance. You can maximize depth of field by focusing at the hyperfocal distance. Then everything from halfway between the camera and that point out to infinity will be in focus. This can be particularly useful when you are shooting big landscapes or scenics with wide-angle lenses or zoom lenses and you want everything from the immediate foreground to the distant background to be in focus.

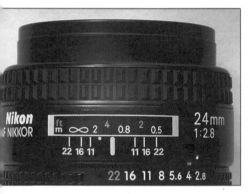

Figure 4-3 Hyperfocal setting on a 24mm lens

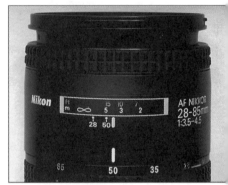

Figure 4-4 Hyperfocal setting at focal length of 50mm on a 28–85mm zoom lens

Table 4-1 gives approximate hyperfocal distances for a typical selection of such focal lengths. First, get the hyperfocal distance for the particular lens length and aperture you are using from the table. Then adjust the focusing ring until the hyperfocal distance on the distance scale lines up with the distance index line. For example, using a 24mm lens with the aperture set to f/22 as shown in Figure 4-3, the hyperfocal distance is about 3 feet, which means that, when focused to 3 feet, everything from 1¹/₂ feet in front of the camera out to infinity will be in focus.

With a zoom lens, set the focal length and aperture first, then set the focus to the hyperfocal distance for that particular focal length and aperture combination. For example, the zoom lens in Figure 4-4 is set to a focal length of 50mm and an aperture of f/22. Using Table 4-1, focus the lens to 13 feet to maximize depth of field between 6¹/₂ feet from the camera out to infinity. If your lens does not have a depth-of-field scale, which many zooms lack, use hyperfocal tables to precisely control the depth of field.

Table 4-1. Approximate Hyperfocal Distances*

Focal length	f/8	f/11	f/16	f/22	f/32
20	6	4	3	2	1½
24	8	6	4	3	2
28	11	8	6	4	3
35	17	12	10	7	5
50	34	25	18	13	10
70	67	50	34	24	17
85	99	72	50	36	25

*Note: All distances are in feet.

The physics of lenses dictate that apertures in the middle range of f-stops, between f/8 and f/11, will produce the sharpest overall images—this range is known as the lens's "sweet spot." To maximize the sharpness of your photographs, use your lens's "sweet spot" whenever possible. Avoid using a very small aperture, f/16 or smaller, unless you absolutely need the extra depth of field, such as in a big landscape where you want both the foreground and background to be in focus. And avoid using a large aperture, f/5.6 or larger, unless you absolutely need the extra light, such as when shooting action at higher shutter speeds or in low-light conditions.

> **TIP**
> Use f/8 or f/11 unless you need maximum depth of field or a very fast shutter speed.

Zoom lenses have a second "sweet spot" to consider. Just as the middle apertures produce the sharpest images with any lens, the middle focal lengths of a zoom's range also produce sharper images than focal lengths at either end of the range. If you find yourself at the far end of your zoom, like the 210mm end of a 70mm–210mm zoom, move closer to your subject if possible and back off the focal length. Likewise, at the near end, move further back if possible and zoom in with the lens.

Zooming

Any lens can be a "zoom" lens. If your lens is a real zoom lens with a range of focal lengths, then zoom the lens in and out to get the best composition. They are great for filling the frame with your subject and eliminating background clutter.

However, if you are using a fixed focal length lens, you can still zoom but *you* have to do the zooming. Move closer to fill the frame with your subject, move back to include more of the subject's surroundings, or move around to get a better angle of view. In any case, do not just stand where you are and snap away. Move around and "zoom" in and out with your feet to get the best composition.

FILTERS

A filter can be added to your lens to manipulate the light striking the film and thus create different effects in the resulting photograph. Myriad filters are available today that can create myriad effects, from turning a point of light into a brilliant star burst to filling a clear sky with fog to making sunset seem like late morning. However, these effects are too unnatural for most nature and adventure photographers and, for as little as you would use them, they are usually not worth the extra bulk or expense. Only a handful of filters are really necessary to solve a few key problems and produce better color outdoor photographs. These include *ultraviolet (UV)* or skylight, warming, polarizing, and neutral-density filters.

Round filters screw onto the front of your lens; thus, you buy each filter to fit your particular lenses. However, if you have a variety of lenses that take different-diameter filters, this can get quite expensive. To reduce cost and the amount of gear you have to carry, buy one filter set that fits your largest lens and a set of step-up rings that allows you to adapt them to lenses with smaller diameters. To save time, also buy a set of lens caps that fits that filter set. Leave the step-up rings attached to each lens and cover with the bigger lens cap. Then you can quickly switch filters between different-sized lenses.

The use of filters is not limited to 35mm SLR cameras. Several manufacturers make filter holders that can be mounted onto compact point-and-shoot cameras as well. With such a holder, any of the filters described here can be used with a point-and-shoot camera. However, using filters that reduce the light entering the lens, such as a polarizing filter, is only practical with point-and-shoot cameras that have through-the-lens (TTL) light-metering. And because you cannot look through the lens of most point-and-shoot cameras as you can with SLR cameras, you will not have quite the creative control that an SLR provides.

Ultraviolet, haze, and skylight filters. The ubiquitous *ultraviolet (UV), haze,* and *skylight filters* are probably the most overused and least understood filters used by outdoor photographers. One or the other is often recommended as permanent lens protection from drops and bumps, but adding another layer of glass can increase flare. If your purpose in adding such a filter is protection, use a lens hood instead, which provides better protection and actually reduces flare. Why use one of these filters? They are useful in keeping spray or dust off of your lens, especially during storms. All three will reduce the amount of ultraviolet light that reaches the film, which you do not see but the film records as a slight blu-ish cast. The skylight filter, which is slightly pink, also adds a hint of warmth to the final image. These may be useful in some situations, such as at higher elevations, but should not be used as a permanent extension to your lenses.

Warming filter. Warming filters are, however, much more useful and also provide lens protection. On overcast days or in the shadows on sunny days, the light tends to be bluish and cool. You often do not see this bluish cast because your brain filters it to match your perception of a more natural light. How-ever, your film will record it. The yellow-ish-amber 81 series filters remove this cool, bluish cast, resulting in a warmer, more pleasing photograph. The 81A returns the scene to a more natural color. The stronger 81B, which is the most popu-lar, adds a bit of warmth and brings out the color. The even stronger 81C really heats up an image.

> **TIP**
> Use an 81A warming filter instead of a UV or skylight filter when shooting in shade or under overcast skies.

Polarizing filter. Polarizing filters also solve several frequently encountered light problems and, if used properly, can enhance the color in a scene. Sunlight is reflected by the atmosphere, water, and the objects that we photograph, creating unwanted haze and glare. Polarizers are es-pecially useful when the sun is higher in the sky or your subject is soaked from rain or spray, even on cloudy days. They remove this reflected light, enhancing the color of green vegetation, blue skies, and rainbows, as well as cutting through the haze often found at higher elevations and in reflec-tions off of water.

The effect of a polarizing filter varies depending on the direction you are pointing your lens relative to the direction of the sunlight. The effect is greatest when the camera is aimed at a ninety-degree angle from the sun and least when aimed directly at or away from the sun or under an overcast sky. Be careful when using a wide-angle lens with a polarizer to photograph a scene with lots of blue sky. The sky at right angles to the sun will appear dark blue, while the sky nearest and farthest from the sun will appear light blue, which is not very natural. Also be careful to not over-polarize when photographing at higher altitudes, which can unnatu-rally blacken the sky. If you get this effect and are using the polarizer to cut through haze, turn the polarizer's ring or try an ultraviolet (UV) or haze filter instead.

Polarizers reduce the amount of light reaching the film by up to two stops, which can be a problem when you need to use higher shutter speeds but is useful when you want to slow down the shutter speed in brighter light, such as when shooting waterfalls. So do not use them unless they enhance your photograph. To check what effect one might have, simply hold it in your hand, oriented as if you were about to mount it on your lens. Then turn the outer ring while looking through it to see what happens. If you see an enhancement you like, then take the time to mount it on your lens. Otherwise, put it back in your bag.

Neutral-density filter. Split or graduated neutral-density (N-D) filters, commonly referred to as "grads," are another type of filter worth carrying on every trip. In these rectangular filters, shown at lower right in Figure 4-5, one half is clear and the other half is darker by one, two, or three stops. These useful filters allow you to balance the bright highlights and dark shadows often found in outdoor scenes, such as sunlit peaks and a shadow-filled valley below, or other situations in which the background is bright and the foreground darker.

For example, the photograph in Plate 17 was shot using a graduated N-D filter. In these situations, which are frequently encountered espe-

Figure 4-5
Essential gear (clockwise from top left): extra film, blower brush and microfiber cleaning cloth, extra batteries, filters with step-down rings, shutter release cable, film leader retriever, graduated N-D filter, and lens hood

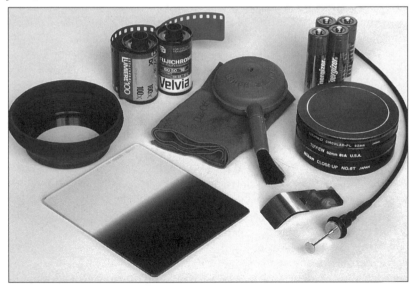

cially early and late in the day, it is impossible to shoot the scene as you see it with slide film, and sometimes even with print film. If you expose for the brightly lit part of the scene, the darker part will be nearly black in the resulting picture. If you expose for the darker part, the well-lit section will become glaringly bright. The only way to shoot a satisfactory image of the entire scene is to expose for the darker part of the scene and use a graduated N-D filter to darken the brighter part.

Using these filters is a little tricky but with practice becomes easy. First, point your camera at the darker part of the scene to determine proper exposure. Then put your camera on a tripod or other camera support—it is harder to do this without one—and focus. Hold the filter in front of your lens so that the darker section covers the brighter part of the scene, usually the sky. To be effective, there should be a line or area across the scene with which you can match the boundary, or gradation, between the dark and clear halves of the filter. Matching this line in the scene with the filter's gradation line without the line actually showing is the tricky part.

To make sure that the filter is positioned properly, hold down your camera's depth-of-field preview button and adjust the filter up or down until positioned the way you want it. Select your lens's smallest aperture, if you are not already using it; then return the aperture to the desired setting after adjusting the filter's position. You may want to bracket your shots with the filter in different positions to get it in the right place. However, avoid shooting at the smallest aperture unless you need to maximize depth of field. By shooting at f/8 or f/11, you will get the best optical sharpness and the filter's gradation line will not be noticeable.

The graduated N-D filter can be handheld, which means you have to keep your fingers out of the way, or in a filter holder, which allows more precise adjustment but is another piece of gear to carry. With practice, handholding is adequate for most situations and eliminates the need to carry the holder. The N-D filters are available in two sizes, with one-, two-, and three-stop differences between the light and dark halves and with either sharp or more gradual boundaries between the halves. Start with a larger, high-quality, two-stop filter with a softer, more gradual boundary. Avoid round, screw-on graduated N-D filters, because you cannot adjust the location of the boundary between the clear and dark halves.

FILM
Selecting Film

As any visit to a camera store will show you, there is a bewildering array of films available today. Most of these films are for specialized applications or for snapshooters. There are only a handful that provide the sharpness, color, and flexibility needed for high-quality outdoor and adventure photography. Unless you are shooting enough to really get to know a variety of films, pick one or two and concentrate on them. Learn their characteristics and when to switch from one to the other.

Prints vs. slides. Your first choice is print (negative) film versus slide (transparency or positive) film. Print film has a number of advantages that make it very popular, especially among snapshooters. First, it is far more forgiving of bad exposure choices than is slide film. An over- or underexposed negative can still produce a satisfactory print. Prints are also much easier for just one or two people to view at once and are fun to arrange in albums that tell a story. However, in the long run, using print film will be more expensive than shooting slides. Plus the printing process takes away some of your creative control. The final outcome is at least to some extent determined by the printer rather than you, sometimes requiring you to work with the printer to get what you want. If you want large display prints, then shoot with print film and find a quality printer.

Slide film, on the other hand, is the choice of the majority of professional and serious outdoor photographers. It is sharper and more color-saturated than print film, as well as cheaper over the long run. Slides are easier for larger groups to view and it is fun to put on slide shows after a potluck dinner. If you hope someday to publish your photographs, keep in mind that virtually all publishers now require transparencies and will only rarely accept prints. When you want a print, you can always make one from a slide, although the print may be a bit more contrasty and intense colors may lose some of their punch when compared to viewing the slide in a projector. However, slide film records a more narrow range of tones than does print film. Shadows and highlights may appear as black-and-white areas in slides but look about right in prints. Consequently, slide film requires more careful and accurate exposure choices.

The final, and perhaps most important, reason to use slide film: we have entered the digital age. Transparencies are better for digital imaging than are prints. Output and image manipulation options for amateurs are rapidly approaching what has only been available for professionals willing to pay the price. For example, imaging centers are now open in most cities where anyone can scan a slide onto a computer, edit the image on computer, and print the final image that looks better than a traditional print at about the same or a slightly higher cost.

Natural vs. saturated color. A variety of both print and slide films are appropriate for outdoor and adventure photography. These tend to fall into two basic categories: films with higher contrast, supersaturated colors, and a hint of warmth, and films with lower contrast, more muted colors, and a neutral to cooler color balance. The former are very popular for most outdoor photography, but the latter may be more appropriate for people's faces, snowscapes, and other situations in which you want even, accurate color rendition. Experiment by shooting several rolls in different situations to determine which you like the best.

Slow vs. fast. As a rule, use the slowest film possible for the situation because sharpness increases as the ISO number decreases. To illustrate, ISO 50 35mm films can make sharp prints up to 20 inches by 24 inches, while ISO 400 films are usually limited to $8\frac{1}{2}$ inches by 11 inches. For most photography, slower films—ISO 100 or less—are by far the most popular among serious and professional outdoor photographers. For wildlife, action, and handheld photography, ISO 50 films pushed one stop or ISO 100 films, which can be pushed to ISO 200, are their first choice. Most pros do not use ISO 400 films. However, today's ISO 400 films are as sharp as ISO 100 films of a decade ago, which were perfectly satisfactory at the time. Try them for action and general, handheld photography, but their increased graininess may be unsatisfactory.

Professional vs. amateur. Many films are available in professional and amateur versions. As with other film options, which works best for you is up to you. Most people cannot tell the difference between identical photographs taken with each type. Virtually no one can tell which type a photograph was taken with by looking at it. That said, fresh, professional films usually perform as expected more consistently. To get the most out of your film and your photo opportunities, use the professional versions. However, amateur versions, which are cheaper, may work just fine for your general-purpose use and for experimentation when you want to save money. Try them both, then decide for yourself.

Storing and Traveling With Film

Storing and traveling with film can be a real challenge. Keep unused film in a dark, cool place, the best of which is your refrigerator or freezer. When traveling, your film faces a gauntlet of radical temperature changes, dirt, and X rays. To save space, remove film rolls from their boxes and canisters, which can be recycled. Carry the rolls in resealable, clear plastic bags, which allow for quick identification by you and quick inspection by airport security guards.

When traveling by car, store film in a cooler if possible. Or bury your film in the middle of your clothes bag, which provides insulation, then keep the bag in the shade.

When traveling by air, hand carry your film if at all possible, avoiding the X ray machine. However, recent tests have shown that a few passes through the machines in more modern airports, which run bags through on a conveyor belt, will not harm film; so do not be too concerned if you cannot avoid them. However, if the machines are the older, large ones into which baggage is loaded, doused with X rays, then removed, ask that your film be hand inspected or put it in lead-lined bags. If you must check your film through as baggage, which is always X rayed, place it in lead-lined pouches in the center of a nondescript bag surrounded by other gear. Although X rays are not likely to cause a problem, quick fingers might. Lock the bag's zippers and wrap duct tape around the bag. Avoid shiny, new bags with a popular brand name emblazoned on the side.

WORKING IN BAD WEATHER

As any outdoorsperson knows, the weather outdoors is usually less than perfect. It is often hot, cold, humid, windy, raining, or snowing. But uncooperative weather conditions should not stop you from photographing. In fact, some of the best images have been taken in such conditions. For example, rain can add a unique softness to landscapes; a brooding storm can produce very evocative images. However, it can be a real challenge to get such images in inclement weather without ruining your camera gear. Your gear can take just about any conditions that you can. But, just as you have to protect yourself from the elements, you must also protect your camera gear appropriately.

Heat

If you can stand the heat outside, then your camera gear probably can too. Even when it is not all that hot, keep your camera out of the direct sunlight as much as possible. Store gear that you are not using inside of a padded pack, case, or bag to prevent the sun's rays from heating black cameras and lenses, and keep the gear that you are using shaded. An umbrella held by an extension arm clamped to your tripod is ideal for keeping both you and your gear cool, or work in the shade whenever possible.

Your film, however, is more sensitive to heat and should be protected more carefully. An insulated soft lunch bag or small cooler with ice will keep a day's worth of film cool while out in the field. Store the rest of your film in a cooler in your car or camp. Even when it is not blazing hot outside, keep your film out of direct sunlight and avoid putting film in the pocket of a jacket or pants made from a dark fabric.

Cold

Working with camera gear in extreme cold is usually tougher on you than your gear. Touching cold metal with bare skin saps heat from your body very quickly, leaving you cold and miserable, and sometimes freezes your skin, causing plenty of pain. Thus, always wear liner gloves while shooting, and slip your hands into pockets or a pair of oversized mittens tied to your jacket in between shots to keep them warm. Be careful to not touch the back of the camera with your cheek while shooting; either wear a face mask or insulate the back of the camera with heavy tape or thin foam. Finally, wrap your tripod's legs with pipe insulation or a commercially available leg wrap.

Weak or inoperative batteries are one of the most common problems encountered in cold weather. Most of your camera gear can take the cold except for batteries. Their capacity diminishes in very cold temperature. Keep extra batteries warm inside your jacket. Once the batteries in your camera get too cold, swap them with the warm set. Alternatively, you can use an external battery pack, which can be kept warm inside your jacket.

Another common problem during cold conditions is condensation, which forms when warm air hits your cold camera. This occurs when you breathe on the camera as well as when you take the camera inside. If you do get condensation, wait until the camera's temperature has restabilized, then gently wipe it off. To prevent condensation while shooting, turn your head to direct your exhalation away from the camera. When you go back inside, put your camera inside a sealable plastic bag, squeeze all the air out, and seal the bag. If you do not have a bag, wrap the camera in your jacket. This will allow the camera to warm up slowly and keep condensation off of the camera itself.

Keeping your camera under clothing and too close to your own body heat can also cause condensation. If it is precipitating or really cold, keep your camera under your first layer or two of clothing, which should offer enough protection without allowing the camera to warm up too much or too quickly.

Precipitation

Do not let precipitation stop you from getting great shots. Most cameras, even the more modern electronic wonders, can take a sprinkling of water and keep on clicking. However, too much precipitation, and even high humidity, can cause problems and ruin camera gear. Always take a few resealable plastic bags and a large plastic garbage bag or two to protect your equipment when conditions are really bad. While shooting in the rain or snow, use a lens hood to keep water off of the front element and drape a garbage bag or one of the commercially available rain covers over your camera. When looking through the viewfinder, stick your head under the cover or roll the cover back to expose the eyepiece. Alternatively, cut a hole in the plastic bag for your lens, then place the camera in the bag with the lens sticking out of the hole. If it is not too windy, an umbrella clamped onto an extension arm clamped to a tripod leg is even better. A clear plastic shower cap placed over the camera body also works well when using shorter lenses.

Water on the outside of your camera is not much of a problem. Simply wipe it away with a chamois or other absorbent cloth. However, water on the inside can be a real problem. Remove the lens and any caps from the camera. Shake out any remaining water or carefully wipe out the inside with a cotton swab. Then store everything in a warm, dry place until all moisture has evaporated. In very humid conditions, such as in rain forests, you will have to create such a place by placing your gear inside a sealed plastic bag or other watertight container with an ample amount of silica gel, which is available from camera stores or chemical supply stores. Once the silica gel has done its job, spread it on a cookie sheet and bake it in the oven at a low temperature before using again.

WORKING WITH FILL FLASH

Most outdoor photographers rely on the sun to provide the primary light for their photographs. Unfortunately, the sun is often less than cooperative in providing the best or even good lighting. For some photographs, like big landscapes, the only alternative is to wait, if possible, until the light changes to suit you. However, when the subject is relatively close to your camera, you can use a *fill flash* to overcome the problems caused by an uncooperative sun or to create images, such as Plate 5, that would not otherwise be possible. This second light source is used to provide fill lighting that complements the light from the primary light source, the sun. It "fills in" poorly lit and shadowy areas, hence the term "fill flash."

In the past, fill flash has been far too complicated for all but the most serious outdoor photographers. However, with recent advances in technology, flash has become a useful and surprisingly simple tool for outdoor photography. In particular, fill flash can enhance your photographs significantly by reducing contrast, stopping action, and warming up your subject. This extends the range of light conditions in which you can take satisfying photos to include severe side- or backlighting, bright sun at high noon, or deep shadows. In addition, fill flash can enhance your creativity, allowing you to capture action and enhance

89

your subject in ways that would not be possible without the flash.

To look natural, the fill light source—your flash—must not over-power the ambient light provided by the sun. Thus, fill flash should, in general, be balanced with the ambient natural light level. Sometimes it should be a bit brighter relative to the ambient light, to make the subject stand out from the background. But usually it should be less bright than the ambient light to leave some shadow on the subject. This balancing is the hard part.

When photographing people or animals, flash can cause the subject's eyes to glow a bright, unnatural red. This problem, called "red eye," is particularly noticeable when photographing in relatively low light levels when your subject's pupils are open. To avoid "red eye," use a flash that has a "red eye" reduction capability, which means that the flash actually fires two or more times. The initial bursts close the subject's pupils; the last burst provides light for the photograph. Additionally, position the flash at an angle relative to your subject. Either attach the flash to a bracket or hold the flash using an extension cord between your camera and flash as described below.

Automatically balanced flash. If your camera is capable of *automatically balanced fill flash* via a built-in flash, like virtually all automatic point-and-shoot cameras made today and some SLRs, or has a separate unit mounted on your SLR camera's hot shoe, then your equipment can do the hard part for you. In general, these flashes are smarter than you are, at least when it comes to estimating flash output. They communicate with the camera to get exposure settings and ambient light level as read by the camera's through-the-lens (TTL) light meter (referred to as TTL flash), and then calculate the appropriate flash output. When you take the picture, the flash reads the light reflecting back to the camera and shuts the flash off when the correct light level has been reached.

If you have one of these smart flashes, just read your owner's manuals, experiment, and let the flash do the work. However, sometimes you have to fool them with a few tricks to get better pictures. Even though balanced, most of these flashes will produce an unnatural-looking image. Flash is direct front-lighting, which, as discussed in chapter 2, can produce flat, unsatisfying photos. Thus, you should reduce the flash output by one to two stops relative to the ambient light level to achieve a more natural look. This will reduce highlights caused by the flash reflecting off bright surfaces, and leave enough shadow to look like you did not use a flash. Consult your flash's manual for details on how to do this, and experiment to learn how much reduction you like the best.

If you want a background that is a little darker, to enhance a foreground subject, then use the fill flash as you normally would but under-expose the background by using matrix or evaluative metering and dialing in exposure compensation in your camera. For example, to underexpose the background by one stop, dial in minus one stop. Also, try dialing in plus one stop on the flash. If you only have center-weighted metering, meter the background and underexpose by one stop and add a stop to your flash setting. Consult your camera's and flash's manuals for further details. If you have a fully automatic camera that you cannot override, like most point-and-shoots, tape a piece of translucent paper over the flash to physically reduce its output.

The light produced by flash is typically balanced to match the color and temperature of bright, midday light. When shooting during daylight hours, this works just fine. However, when shooting early or late in the day, when the natural light is much warmer, this difference can create a very unnatural look. Hold a sunset filter, 85 series gel, or some other warming filter over the flash to better match its output to the color of the natural light.

Through the lens (TTL) flash. You can also use just about any automatic TTL flash unit as a fill flash, even if it does not automatically balance its output as discussed above. Automatic flashes are designed to be used as the primary light source indoors or at night. Thus, to use them effectively as a fill flash in daylight, you must reduce their output. To do this, first determine the proper exposure for the scene you want to shoot as if you were not using flash. If you have a camera with automatic exposure (AE) modes, set it to manual mode. Then set the shutter speed and aperture manually. Make sure you set the aperture big enough for your flash's power and the shutter speed no higher than your camera's maximum shutter speed that can be used with a flash, usually 1/125 or 1/250 second.

If your camera has a built-in TTL flash, increase your camera's ISO setting one to two stops higher (faster), but do not change the aperture or shutter speed settings. This is not the same as pushing your film, so process it normally. Do not forget to reset it when you are done fill flashing. If you have a separate unit, increase the ISO or decrease the f-stop one to two stops on the back of the flash. Consult your flash's manual for the best way to reduce its output, and experiment to find out what works best for you.

Accessories. Moving the flash a foot or two away from the camera, if possible, avoids the harsh front-lighting problem of on-camera flash and may be required if the subject that you want filled in is off center. A number of mounting brackets are available on which you can mount your flash or, if the subject is not moving around, you can simply hold the flash in your hand, aiming it at your subject. Either way you will need a cord between your camera's hot shoe and your flash. Finally, bouncing or diffusing the flash's light will soften its effect and reduce distracting highlights, again often producing a more satisfying result. Several pocket-sized diffusers and reflectors are commercially available, but a white T-shirt, white paper, or aluminum foil will work just fine.

A final note: these flashes are very power hungry, so carry plenty of extra batteries in the field. If possible, carry your flash's manual with you in the field.

CAMERA AND GEAR

Features to look for in a point-and-shoot camera:

+ **weatherproof**
+ **built-in fill flash**
+ **35mm fixed lens or 28mm–105mm zoom**
+ **tripod socket**
+ **accepts screw-in filters**
+ **self-timer**
+ **selectable ISO setting or exposure compensation**

Useful features in a 35mm SLR camera:

+ **automatic and manual exposure**
+ **autowind**
+ **exposure compensation**
+ **spot metering mode**
+ **depth-of-field preview**
+ **auto-balanced TTL fill flash**
+ **interchangeable focusing screens**
+ **self-timer**
+ **cable-release socket**
+ **multiple exposure**

Outdoor and travel photography kit:

+ **35mm SLR camera**
+ **zoom lens in the 28mm–105mm range with hood**
+ **zoom lens in the 70mm–210mm or 70mm–300mm range with hood**
+ **flash with automatically balanced fill-flash capability**
+ **lightweight tripod with ball head**
+ **close-up diopters (see Close-up and Macro Photography, chapter 5)**
+ **circular polarizing and 81B warming filters with step-down rings**
+ **two-stop graduated N-D filter**
+ **shutter release cable**
+ **cleaning kit**
+ **extra film and batteries**
+ **resealable plastic bags and a large plastic garbage bag**

Chapter 5

OUTDOOR ADVENTURE

Outdoor adventure in local parks, remote backcountry, or faraway lands can provide a wide range of unique photo opportunities. The pursuit of adventure often takes you to places with outstanding scenery and wildlife that most people never see and opens a window to exotic, but often disappearing, peoples and cultures that most people only read about. The adventure itself also makes for exciting photographs. Climbing, for example, is full of great shots like a death-defying leap over a crevasse, a seemingly impossible move up an overhanging rock face, or the final struggle to a peak's summit.

Given the photo opportunities that most adventures provide, it is often worth taking the extra steps to make a great photograph rather than grabbing a quick snapshot. The shots you take along the way will last far longer than the adventure itself. Moreover, you spent a lot of time and effort to be there, so taking the care and time to get the photographs that you really want will be worth it in the long run. To get those shots, slow down, take the time to really see what is going on around you, and apply the principles covered in this book. This chapter adds a variety of tips, ideas, and techniques that will help you get better photographs of the people, action, scenery, flora, and fauna experienced on your adventure.

The first step is to take your camera gear and keep it at your fingertips. You cannot take pictures if your camera is buried in your backpack or luggage. Then it is just a question of applying the techniques in this book. Find a worthy subject, which should be easy, and develop an eye-grabbing composition that best shows that subject and eliminates the surrounding clutter. Work the light, getting up early or staying late for the magic hour, looking for the drama of clearing storms, the simple interplay of light and shadow, or the soft, even light of an overcast day. Use your equipment as a creative tool, not just a recorder. But remember, adventuring can be hazardous, and taking pictures can make it more so. Focus first on your own safety, and second on getting good photographs.

Most adventures keep you moving and end far too soon, which means you often have limited time for photography. To make the most of the time that you do have, think about the shots you want to get prior to the trip and while traveling. Then watch for opportunities along the way to get those shots. Working out the shots well before you actually take them can save a lot of time and film while you are out there. Advance research can also save time when adventuring in new and unfamiliar locations. Look through travel guides, magazines, and coffee-table books to get ideas for locations and compositions. Once you get there, look at postcards and promotional literature for additional information and ideas. Ask residents and other travelers for information; they are often more than happy to let you in on local secrets that are not included in guidebooks.

TELL A STORY

The shots that we take often become slide shows at post-adventure potluck dinners, fill scrapbooks, or grace our walls. Through them we get to relive the adventure and share it with others. So telling a story is often a big part of adventure photography. Two guidelines can help you tell a more entertaining and memorable story.

First, do not try to cover the whole experience in one or two shots. Rather, take a collection of photographs, each of which tells a single part or aspect of that story. When composing each shot, think of how the composition communicates its part of the story and how it fits into the story as a whole.

And second, when deciding what to photograph, treat your story like an adventure movie that includes all the important pieces and nothing more. Start with shots that show the adventure's setting, including how you got there, especially if it is something as exotic as a camel train, and your starting point. Include any recognizable landmarks or features, such as a Buddhist monastery or well-known peak, to give your story a place. Then peel back a layer to show the details of that place and the adventure itself, including smaller-scale scenic shots, slices of life along the way, and

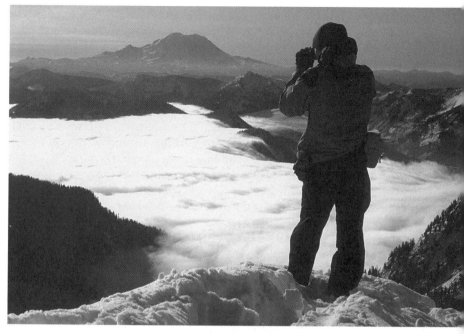

Figure 5-1 Photographing Red Mountain, Washington

the action itself, as well as close-ups of people and whatever defines their culture or activity. You might try switching back and forth between the adventure itself and the surrounding environment. End the story with some logical conclusion such as a triumphant return to base camp or the farewell party prior to returning home.

Adding People

People, their activities, and the trappings of their culture are an important, if not the most important, aspect of our adventures. In adventure shots, people themselves or their emotions and actions can be the subject of a photograph such as the "Sing Sing" dancers in Plate 21. Or they

TIP

When including people in your photograph, have them looking at you when they are the subject; otherwise, have them look away from the camera toward the subject.

can be a supporting element that increases the viewers' involvement with the scene, often evoking an "I wish I was there" reaction, such as the person standing among the wildflowers in Plate 8.

Either way, including people in your photograph has a powerful impact on its composition. For example, viewers will follow their line of

95

sight to see what they are looking at and their line of travel to see where they are going. Viewers will also be immediately drawn to faces to see if they are recognizable and to read the emotions revealed in their expressions. So be careful how you incorporate people into your pictures. When included appropriately, people make high-impact subjects and can play a strong supporting role, but if not, they can detract from an otherwise good composition.

People as part of a scene. When the objective of your photograph is to show the scenery in which your adventure is taking place or the adventure in the context of the surrounding environment, then include people as a supporting element, such as the Penan hunters in the rain forest in Plate 22. When they are close to you and will be larger in the photograph, use a wide-angle lens and place them in the foreground or off to one side as they look into the scene. Their presence will provide the viewer with a sense of scale and draw the viewer into the scene. Avoid showing faces that will draw attention away from the subject. Rather, have them looking at whatever they are doing or toward the subject itself. Try shots with people perched on the edge of a cliff or standing on a summit gazing out at the scenery beyond, as in Figure 5-1.

Figure 5-2 Kayaker, Alaska

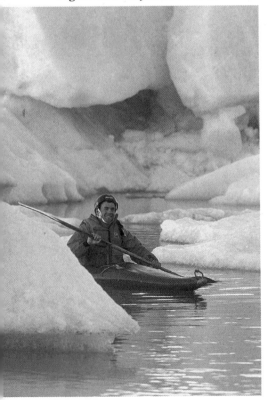

People as the subject. On the other hand, when your objective is to show the people themselves, then they should clearly be the subject of the image. Fill the viewfinder with them as in Plate 18 of the Kayapo Indian mother and child. At least make them large enough in the photograph so their faces and actions are clearly visible. When people are relatively large in the scene and facing the camera, focus on the face and try to show their facial expressions. People's emotions are often a big part of any adventure, and their expressions will communicate the

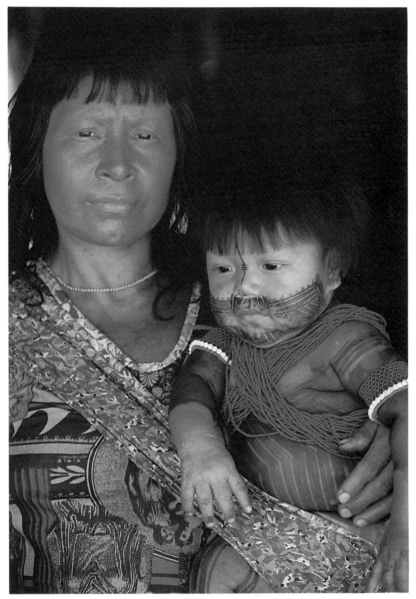

Plate 18 Kayapo Mother and Child, Xingu River Region, Brazil

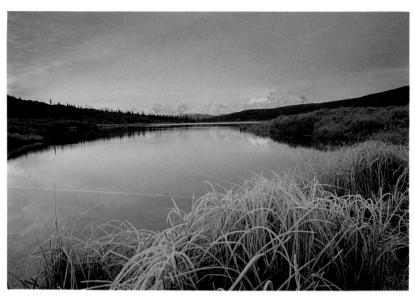

Plate 19

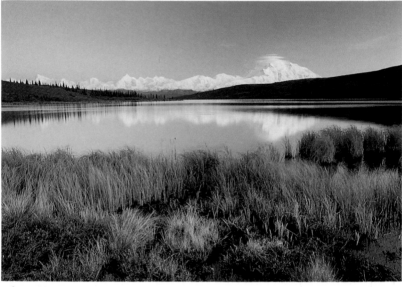

Plate 20

Plates 19 and 20 Wonderlake, Denali National Park, Alaska

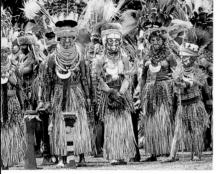

Plate 21

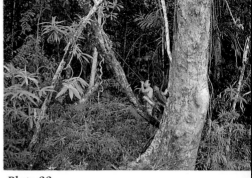

Plate 22

Plate 21 "Sing Sing" Dancers, Papua New Guinea

Plate 22 Penan Hunters, Sarawak Rain Forest, Borneo

Plate 23 Dani Tribespeople, Highlands of Irian Jaya, Indonesia

Plate 24 *Adventuress*, Queen Charlotte Islands, British Columbia, Canada

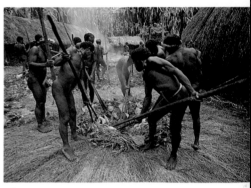

Plate 23

Plate 24

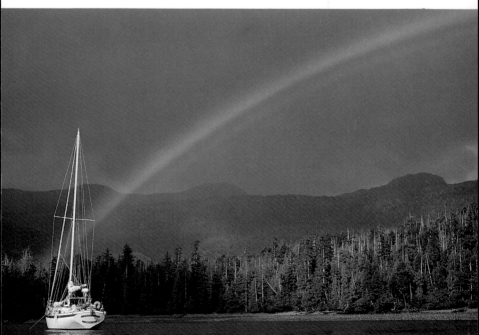

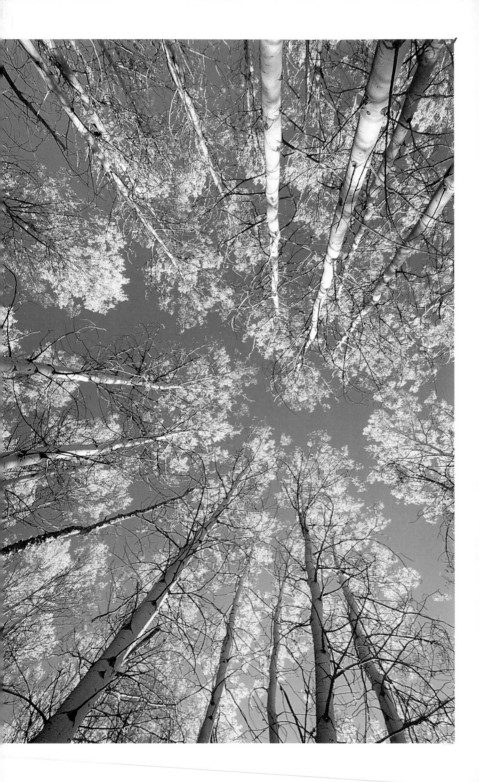

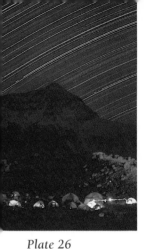 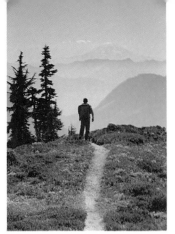 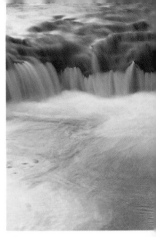

Plate 26   Plate 27   Plate 28

Plate 29

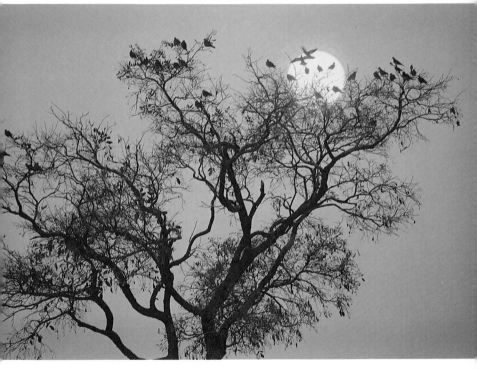

Plate 25 *facing page:* Aspens, Banff National Park, Alberta, Canada

Plate 26 Star Trails Over Camp, Tibet, China

Plate 27 Hiker, Mount Rainier National Park, Washington

Plate 28 Reflections, Escalante River, Utah

Plate 29 Sunset, Okavango Delta, Botswana

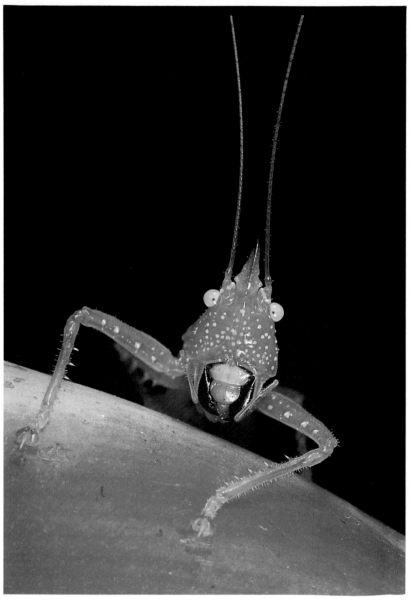

Plate 30 Succulent Katydid, Tambopata River Region, Peru

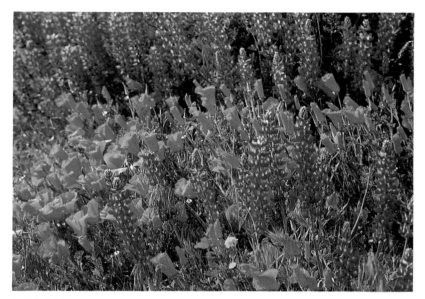

Plate 31

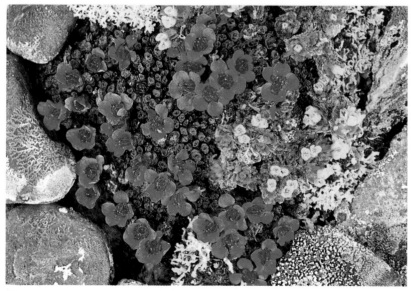

Plate 32

Plate 31 Poppies and Lupine, Central Coast, California
Plate 32 Saxifrage, Somerset Island, Northwest Territories, Canada

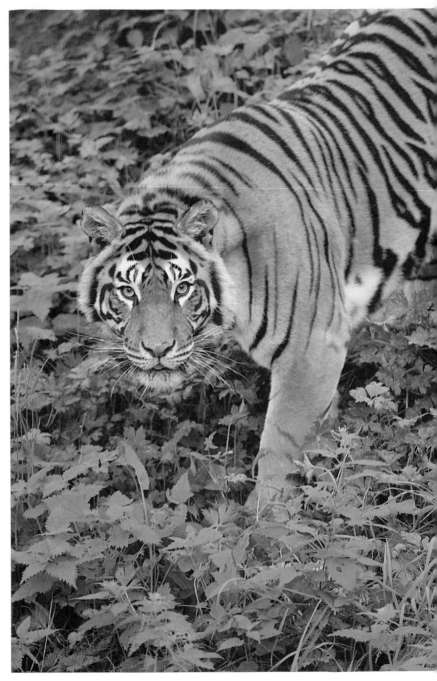

Plate 33 Tiger, India

emotion that they are experiencing, such as the kayaker enjoying himself in Figure 5-2. Capturing the tension on a climber's face after a tough move or the exuberance on the faces of rafters having just made it through a tumbling stretch of white water can add a lot of drama to both the image itself and the story you are trying to tell. However, a relatively large face that is in full view but out of focus can detract significantly from your composition. When you want to emphasize your subjects' activity rather than the subjects themselves, have them look at what they are doing rather than at the camera, such as the Dani tribespeople in Plate 23.

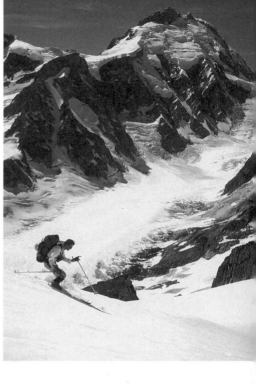

> **TIP**
> When showing people in action, shoot from behind them, placing them low in the frame moving upward and away from you, or in front of them, placing them high in the screen moving downward and toward you.

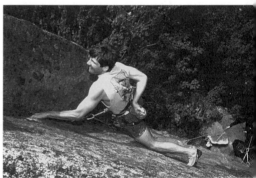

top: *Figure 5-3 Skier*
above: *Figure 5-4 Climber*

People in action. When shooting action, try positioning people in one of two ways—moving into the frame, showing where they are going, or moving out of the frame, showing where they have been. A diagonal line of travel will enhance the sense of movement as in Figure 5-3. For example, a hiker could be positioned in a lower corner of the image, with the trail ahead of him or her leading toward the upper part of the image. Or, when shooting with a wide-angle lens to

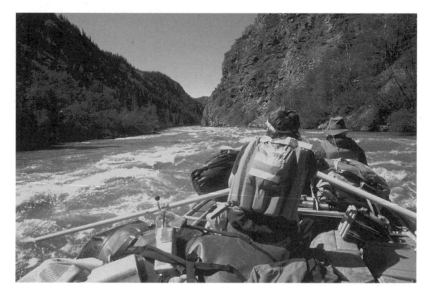

Figure 5-5 Rafters, Tatshenshini River, Yukon, Canada

accentuate the vertical, place a climber high in the frame with the rope trailing down the image toward the belayer at the bottom of the pitch, as in Figure 5-4.

Try shots with your subject just in front of you, positioned low in the frame, as if you are looking over his or her shoulder, such as the rafters in Figure 5-5 or the mountain biker in Figure 5-6. This perspective gives your viewer the feeling that he or she is along on the adventure with you. Alternatively, put your subjects high in the frame with their line of travel in front of them, as with the rafters in Figure 5-7, or put them in the middle with the trail behind them and great scenery beyond, as in Plate 27. For "in-your-face" action, try a wide-angle lens, have your subject moving right at you or just to one side, and wait until the last second before pressing the shutter release button, as in Figure 5-8.

To create a dark backdrop against which to shoot the action, position yourself across from a sunny spot with a deep shadow behind it. Determine exposure in the sunny area, using a shutter speed to get the effect of motion that you want (see Table 1-1, chapter 1). Then shoot your subjects with a telephoto lens as they emerge from the shadows into the sun.

Using fill flash while shooting action at slower shutter speeds, like 1/30 second, can create some interesting effects, as in Figure 5-9. Your picture will still have the impression of action and speed, but all or part of your subject will be frozen inside the whir of motion. The flash also puts a catch-light, a tiny reflection of the flash's light, in the subject's eyes, which adds more life to the photograph.

For best results, use rear-curtain synchronization if your equipment has that capability. Normally, the flash fires just as the shutter begins to open. In rear-curtain synch mode, the flash

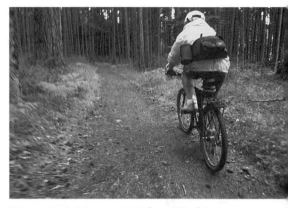

Figure 5-6 Mountain Biker, Washington

fires as it closes, which leaves a trail of motion behind the subject. Consult your flash's and camera's manuals to understand how to do this with your system.

Your campsite can provide a number of unique images. To shoot fireside scenes, put your camera on a tripod, compose the image, and focus. Then remove the camera from the tripod and move the camera close enough to fill the middle of the frame with an object, such as a person's face, that is reflecting the warm glow of the firelight. Set the exposure, return

Figure 5-7 White-water Rafting, Tatshenshini River, Yukon, Canada

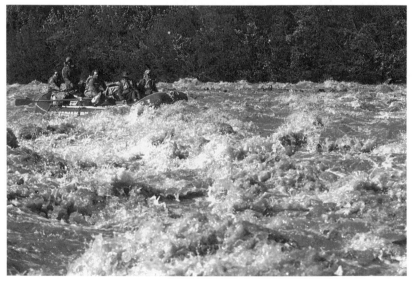

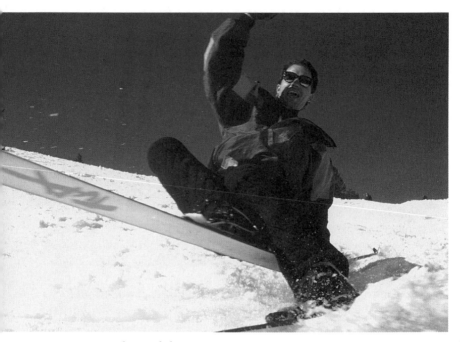

Figure 5-8 Skier, Idaho

the camera to the tripod, and, using a cable release or self-timer, shoot. If you have trouble determining exposure, try a shutter speed of 1/2 second and an aperture of f/5.6 using ISO 100 film.

Combining a flash with the techniques for night scenes (see The Sun, Moon, and Stars, later in this chapter) can result in creative images. An illuminated tent in the foreground with peaks warmed by alpenglow, star streaks, or a full moon in the background is a favorite outdoor image and easy to shoot. To shoot a glowing tent at dusk or night, like Plate 26, simply put someone in the tent with a flash and shoot the scene as you would without the tent being lit. While the shutter is open, have the person inside the tent pop the flash once or twice, being careful not to point the flash at the camera, then close the shutter. For best results, the tent should be in a foreground that is much darker than the background. Other eerie scenes can be created by using the flash, or even a flashlight, in the same way to light up objects in a dark foreground.

When people's faces are not visible or people are relatively small in the scene, they are recognizable by their shapes or forms. Be sure to distinctly show that shape; do not lose it by having all or part of it merging into some other object. For example, heads and necks often get lost in a backpack that protrudes above the shoulders. The compression effect of telephoto lenses can magnify this problem. Check the background to make sure there is no object of a similar tone behind the subjects into which they will merge in the resulting photograph. To make people really stand out, have them wear bright, contrasting colors such as yellow or red. Many professional adventure photographers even carry a packable red windbreaker for just that purpose.

Be careful how you position people near the camera when shooting with a wide-angle lens. The distorting effect of a wide-angle lens will make whatever is closest to the camera appear much bigger relative to the rest of their bodies. Unless you want the distortion, position them farther from the camera, or keep their bodies in a single plane parallel to the camera. Avoid having them sticking an arm back toward the camera or bending over with their backsides toward the camera, which will make them appear unflatteringly large. For example, when photographing climbers, shoot down or across to them, avoiding the inevitably bad "butt shot" from below.

When traveling in unfamiliar lands, be sensitive to the values and mores of the local people. Avoid being too obtrusive or too sneaky. Even

Figure 5-9 Mountain Bikers, Washington

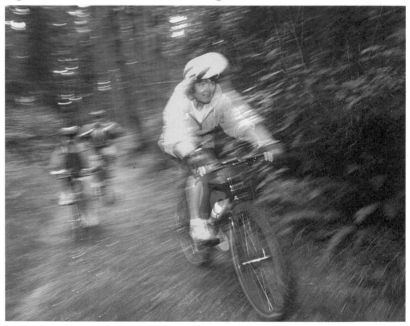

in societies in which photography is familiar and accepted, people may feel that you are invading their privacy and mistrust your presence. Always ask permission to take close-up photographs of people. If your potential subject declines, respect his or her wishes. If a subject asks for a copy, record his or her address and do not forget to send it. In many places, especially those with plenty of tourist traffic, payment may be requested. If you feel that your subjects are indeed providing you a service, then a small gratuity or donation may be just fine. On the other hand, if they are obviously trying to take advantage of you or you simply cannot afford their request, then thank them and find something else to photograph.

Once you have your subjects' permission, then gain their acceptance. When you approach people with a camera, their first instinct is to either hide or pose, neither of which makes for great images. Give them time to relax as well as get to know you and your intentions. Even if you are posing your subjects, allow them time to work into the situation and develop a more natural position. Keep a comfortable distance away from your subjects by using a medium-length telephoto lens. Otherwise your subjects will be too affected by the presence of the camera, which compromises your objective. Once they forget about you and your camera, you will usually get better photographs.

PHOTOGRAPHING LANDSCAPES AND SCENICS

When shooting open landscapes with a wide-angle lens, put something interesting in the foreground to provide a sense of scale and a connection between the viewer and the landscape, such as the moose antlers in Plate 6. Use a small aperture, f/16 or smaller, to ensure enough depth of field to keep both foreground and background in focus (see chapter 4). Wildflowers, animals, weathered wood, rocks, even people can work. Use lines, either implied such as a person's line of sight as in Figure 5-1, or explicit such as the cracks in the mud in Plate 12, to lead your viewer through the image toward the subject. However, be sure not to overwhelm the image with a foreground element that distracts the viewer from the landscape itself.

Do not limit yourself to wide-angle lenses when shooting landscapes; medium to long focal-length lenses can also produce very pleasing, but different, images. Shorter focal length, or wide-angle, lenses open up a scene and emphasize its vastness. Longer focal lengths, on the other hand, compress the elements in a scene, giving the resulting image a more intimate feel.

TIP

When shooting landscapes with a wide-angle lens, include something interesting in the foreground and use an aperture of f/16 or smaller.

This compression can be used, for example, to make a building storm cloud appear to loom broodingly above a farmhouse or town in the foreground. Telephotos are also a great way to extract interesting compositions from a landscape, to eliminate distracting clutter, and to isolate one particular subject within a bigger scene.

If your image has a horizon line, position it to best support the composition. At minimum, make sure that it is parallel to the bottom of the frame. Even a slightly slanted horizon line that obviously should be straight is very distracting. Focusing screens with an architectural grid and small bubble levels that attach to your camera's hot shoe can help align your camera. Place the horizon high in the image when you want to emphasize the foreground and low in the image when you want to emphasize the background or the sky itself. Avoid placing it in the middle of the image, which creates a more static image, much like putting your subject right in the middle. However, there are times when a middle placement makes sense, such as when shooting a subject and its reflection, or when there is something interesting in both the foreground and background as in Plate 28.

TIP

When shooting a colorful sky around sunrise and sunset, try underexposing one-third to one stop to deepen colors in a scene, or overexposing to create pastel colors.

Excessive contrast is a problem in many landscape and scenic shots, especially during the midday hours, when there are deep shadows and bright highlights. Many landscape scenes have a relatively bright upper half, usually filled with sky or brightly lit by the sun, and a darker lower section unlit by the sun or still in the shadows. This is common, for example, when the low-angled sun casts its warm light on the peaks of a mountain landscape but not the foreground or valleys between the peaks. The difference in brightness between the well-lit peaks and the dark foreground often exceeds the range of film, creating a vexing exposure problem.

There are three ways to handle such excessive contrast. First, put as much of the scene's lighter part in the frame as you can and expose for that lighter part, perhaps underexposing by a half stop to better saturate the scene's colors. The darker parts of the scene will recede into blackness in the resulting photograph.

Alternatively, put as much of the scene's darker part in the frame as you can and expose for this darker section. The lighter parts will be a distracting white highlight in the resulting photograph, so eliminate as much of the brighter parts as possible. The first approach is usually better unless you can completely eliminate the distracting brighter section.

The third approach is to use a split or graduated neutral-density filter if feasible (see chapter 4). These filters cut the amount of light from the brighter part of the scene, thus balancing the contrast between bright and dark sections.

Forests and Foliage

Taking pictures inside a forest can be a real challenge. Light levels drop considerably between the forest canopy and floor, making tripods or fast film, or both, essential. Plus sunlight peeks through the canopy, creating high contrast with deep shadows and bright highlights, especially in the canopy itself. To make the most effective images, shoot on overcast days when the contrast and deep shadows found inside the forest are reduced, such as in Plate 16. The right exposure for the forest interior will turn even the smallest patches of sky into very distracting highlights. Worse, the sky may fool your camera's light meter, resulting in an underexposed scene. Aim your camera low to keep the sky out of the picture as in Plate 17.

> **TIP**
>
> **When shooting inside of forests, aim the camera low to eliminate the sky peeking through the canopy and include something colorful such as a person with a red jacket.**

Use an 81A or 81B warming filter even on sunny days to counteract the bluish cast to the reflected light bouncing around inside the forest. Such filters bring out the colors of the foliage, especially fall reds and yellows. Foliage itself is also quite reflective, especially when wet, which can wash out the colors within the forest. Use a polarizer to eliminate this glare and better saturate colors. Unfortunately, this also cuts one to two stops of light, making a tripod essential.

Forests can be a jumble of chaos that seems impenetrable. But a good photographer somehow finds order and creates good compositions. Look for silhouetted shapes of trees, as in Plate 29, patterns in the repetitions of tree trunks, as well as the textures of the trunks themselves. Layers of mist can create a sense of mystery and depth as well as hide much of the chaos, such as the Costa Rican cloud forest in Plate 17. Use medium-length telephotos to extract simpler images from the forest, or wide-angles to open up the forest.

The high contrast found inside the forest can also be used to your advantage. Bring colors and brighter objects forward by using darker shadows, which will go completely black, as a backdrop and interject some color. Most forests are monotonously green and brown. When shooting forest interiors, find a colorful wildflower or put a person dressed in red or yellow in the foreground, looking into the forest.

Fall, with its riot of color, provides incredible photo opportunities. You can shoot close-ups of bright red or yellow leaves against a green, out-of-focus backdrop or big landscapes showing the patterns of color on distant hillsides with individual trees in the foreground. Use warming and polarizing filters, even on overcast days, as well as a highly saturated film to make the fall colors really pop out.

TIP

To saturate the colors of vegetation, use a polarizing filter.

Backlighting can make fall colors look as if they are almost on fire. Try taping a colorful leaf on a window and shooting it with the sun directly behind. To shoot bigger scenes with a wide-angle lens, put colorful trees in the foreground between you and the sun. Or shoot hillsides full of color with a telephoto when the sun is low in the sky and opposite your position. Meter on the foliage itself as a medium tone and keep the sky out of the scene. Shade the front of your lens with your hand or hat to prevent flare.

Snowscapes

Like forest scenes, capturing satisfying snowscapes is a challenge because of the excessive contrast between white snow and deep shadows, as well as because of the way your camera's meter works. Photographing when the light is the most even, such as on overcast days as well as early or late in the day, produces the best results. Use a low-contrast film with a neutral to cooler color bias to ensure white snow and reduce contrast in your photograph.

Exposure on snow can be tricky. If the frame is mostly filled with snow and you use the exposure indicated by your camera's light meter, the snow will be gray in the resulting picture. People's faces and other light- to mid-toned objects will also be underexposed. To ensure a proper exposure, meter highlighted snow and open up one to two stops. One to one and a half stops will preserve detail in the snow but lose detail in the shadows and dark objects. Two stops will produce bright white snow, without detail, and leave more detail in darks. Experiment to get a feel for the difference and see what you you like best. The same techniques also apply to scenes filled with light-colored sand, such as dunes or beaches.

Making a Blue Sky Blue

Washed-out skies are the scourge of many otherwise good photographs. Several techniques can really bring out the blue in the sky.

First, use a polarizing filter, which eliminates the scattered white light that washes out the blue. For best results, keep the sun at your left or right shoulder and be careful at higher elevations, where a polarizing filter can make the sky go almost black. Haze and UV filters also work, especially at higher elevations.

Second, use a film with saturated colors that brings out the blue in the sky. Third, meter on the medium tone of the blue sky itself, well away from the sun, or try underexposing a half stop, which will darken the sky. Finally, choose the right times and places: shoot early or late in the day and away from cities, where increased pollution scatters light even more.

Cloudy-bright conditions are ideal for landscape photography. However, the sky itself will be a big, bright highlight in your photograph that will detract from the composition. Thus, you should minimize or eliminate the sky when it is overcast but bright. If the sky is unavoidable and it is two or more stops brighter than the rest of the picture, then use a split neutral-density filter to even out the contrast. This can also create a more brooding or stormy feeling in your photograph.

The Drama of Bad Weather

Lightning storms are best shot against a dark sky of twilight or night. Before shooting, watch the lightning, noting where it is striking and how frequently and the time between bolts, so that you can anticipate where to aim your camera and when to open the shutter. Reacting to the lightning usually will not work; it will be gone by the time the shutter opens. With your camera and a normal to wide-angle lens mounted on a tripod, compose your image with some foreground and plenty of dark sky, focus at the hyperfocal distance for your lens or at infinity, set the shutter speed to "B," and select a relatively large aperture such as f/5.6 with ISO 50 to ISO 100 film or f/8 with ISO 200 film.

Anticipating the next strike, open the shutter using a shutter release cable long enough to record several strikes, usually 10 to 30 seconds. If it is really dark out, you can leave the shutter open for longer periods to record multiple strikes, covering the front of the lens in between strikes. During the day, add a polarizing filter to darken the scene sufficiently. Use a lens shade and umbrella if it is raining to keep water off the lens and camera. This technique also works well for fireworks and night traffic.

To show the rain itself, position yourself so the rain is strongly backlit or sidelit, preferably against a darker background. Try underexposing by one-half to one stop to let the rain really stand out. Use a shutter speed of 1/125 second to show the raindrops, or 1/30 second or slower to get backlit streaks. Rain softens scenes photographed at very slow shutter speeds, often creating unique images.

When the sun comes out during or at the end of a storm, lighting conditions can be intensely dramatic, especially late or early in the day. The light itself can take on unusual colors and create unusual patterns on the landscape. Look for subjects lit by this intense side- or front-lighting with dark, purple clouds as a backdrop. Meter on the subject or parts of the scene in the sunlight, letting the unlit background become broodingly dark. Also look for crepuscular rays piercing the cloud cover as it breaks apart.

Rainbows are a delightful side effect of clearing storms, morning mist, and waterfalls. Meter the sky and either side of the rainbow and underexpose by one-half to one stop to saturate the colors in the rainbow. If the sky behind the rainbow is very dark, underexpose by one to one and a half stops. Use a polarizing filter to make the rainbow really stand out with richer colors, but be careful to not overpolarize and lose the rainbow. To get an entire rainbow in a 35mm frame, use an ultrawide-angle lens of 20mm or shorter.

The Sun, Moon, and Stars

Including the sun in a photograph can make great images like Plate 29, but determining exposure with the sun in the image can be tricky. If the sun is in the middle of the image or is a large part of the overall scene, it may overpower your camera's meter. To meter properly, swing the camera to the left or right of the sun, eliminating it from the frame. Determine exposure and move the camera back into position. Bracketing will produce lighter and darker images with very different effects. From the original exposure, underexpose by one-half to one stop to saturate the colors, creating a darker, more moody image, or overexpose by one-half to one stop for a lighter, more delicate quality.

To make the sun as big as possible, use a telephoto lens, as big as you have or can create with teleconverters, when the sun is very low in the sky. Set the aperture wide open; the sun may turn into an unnatural polygon if you use any other aperture. Then focus on a subject in the foreground with hard edges such as a tree or a deer. The result will be a striking silhouette against a large sun.

Sunbursts, as in Figure 5-10, are also an intriguing addition to a scenic shot and are easy to photograph. First, use a fixed-focal-length lens—zooms usually cause too much flare—and set the aperture to the smallest

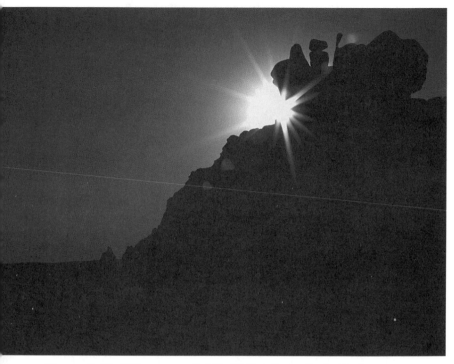

Figure 5-10 Silhouettes, Goblin Valley State Park, Utah

f-stop. Then position yourself so you barely see the sun peeking out behind whatever you are photographing. Set the exposure to get the image you want, making sure that the sun does not overwhelm the meter reading.

Shooting the full moon is also quite easy. For a sharp moon with detail, shoot on a clear night with a mid-range aperture setting and the fastest possible shutter speed (remember, the moon is a moving target). With a telephoto lens, try f/8 at 1/125 second with ISO 100 film and bracket one-half to one stop.

If the moon is not situated in the right position, move it with a double exposure. In the first exposure, photograph the moon as described above with a telephoto lens, positioning it in the frame where you want it in the final image. Include only the moon and the black sky, which will not be exposed in this shot. Then, photograph the second scene, keeping in mind where the moon will be in that image. Determine exposure for the second shot as you normally would without the moon, perhaps underexposing by one-half to one stop if the scene is relatively bright. For best results, the area in the second exposure where the moon will be should be very dark. In between exposures, you can change lenses, add filters, or reposition to get the final image that you want. For example, use a long telephoto for a big, imposing moon, then switch to a wide angle and recompose for the second exposure. Rising full moons at sunset and setting moons at sunrise create very dramatic landscapes. The combination of a full moon low in the sky and a scene lit by the warm light of a sun low in the opposite sky is powerful. A scene with a rising moon is best shot around sunset on the day before the full moon. A scene with a setting moon is best shot around sunrise on the day after it is full. Consult the local newspaper for the date of the full moon as well as times of moonrise and -set. Determine exposure as you would any other front-lit scene.

Scenes lit by the light from a full moon, but without the moon in the frame, can create eerie and haunting photographs. Try a shutter speed of 8 minutes and an aperture of f/4 with ISO 100 film. If there is a lot of snow or clouds in the scene making the scene lighter, halve the shutter speed to 4 minutes. If the moon is less than full, leave the shutter open for 12 to 16 minutes depending on its brightness. Bracket to ensure you get a good exposure.

To create a sky full of star trails, like Plate 26, pick a clear night with no moon or clouds, away from bright city lights. For star circles in the Northern Hemisphere, aim the camera at the North Star, which is in the Little Dipper; in the Southern Hemisphere, aim at the Southern Cross. With your camera mounted on a tripod, compose your image before it gets too dark to see. Set the focus at the hyperfocal distance or at infinity, the aperture to the largest opening (smallest f-stop number), and the shutter speed to "B," and attach a locking shutter release cable. Finally, put a hood on the lens and a plastic bag (shower caps work well for this) over your camera to keep dew off. Then wait.

Several hours after sunset, when the night sky is darkest and the stars brightest, open the shutter by depressing the cable release and locking it down. Leave the shutter open for an extended period, from 15 minutes to 6 hours. Shorter periods turn the stars into streaks, while longer exposures create long curves or circles. It takes about 2 to 3 hours to make complete circles when using a telephoto lens, and 5 to 6 hours with a wide-angle lens. To protect your camera from moisture, leave the plastic bag on the camera but not covering the front of your lens. The lens hood will keep moisture off the glass.

You can create interesting star streak compositions in a variety of ways. First, include objects in the foreground, such as trees, rock formations, or even mountains, that will make silhouetted shapes in shorter exposures or dimly lit forms in longer exposures. To incorporate mountains lit by alpenglow, make a double exposure. Shoot the first one after sunset when alpenglow is at its peak, exposing normally, perhaps underexposing by one-half to one stop to darken the alpenglow's red. Then cover the lens. When the sky is completely dark, remove the cover to add the star trails. Use the same approach to put a firelit scene in the darkness below a sky filled with star trails.

Finally, include tents, people, cactus, or other smaller but interesting objects in the foreground below the night sky, as in Plate 26. Then, while the shutter is open recording the star trails, paint whatever is in the foreground with light. When using a flash, point the unit, not connected to the camera, at the object and fire away. One or two pops may be sufficient. When including tents, pop the flash inside the tent. When using a flashlight, shine the light on the subject, moving it around to shower it completely with light for several minutes. The amount of light will depend on how close the light source is and how dark the objects are. Experiment on a dark night in your backyard to determine how much light to use.

Capturing eerie images of the pulsating Northern (or Southern) Lights is essentially the same as shooting lightning. Put your camera on a tripod, open the aperture wide open, focus to infinity, and set the shutter speed to "B." With a cable release, open the shutter for 15 to 45 seconds with ISO 50 film or 8 to 30 seconds with ISO 100 film.

Reflections and Waterfalls

Reflections can make interesting images in both calm and running water. In still water, try placing the horizon or the line between the subject and its reflection in the middle of the frame, but with the subject off center. Avoid cutting off part of the subject or reflection if possible. Move closer or farther from the water as well as lowering or raising your camera to get the right amount of the reflection in the frame. If you cannot get all of both the subject and its reflection, try removing the subject completely to create an interesting abstraction in which the subject is in the image without actually being there. Reflections in pools or puddles are great for this, especially if the reflection is much brighter than the surrounding area, which will then appear as a dark frame around the subject's reflection.

Rapidly moving water distorts reflections, transforming them from recognizable objects to interesting abstractions filled only with shapes, patterns, and colors like Plate 28. Look for reflections of golden sunlit rocks, bright green foliage, a tree full of red leaves, or some other interesting but distorted subject, and photograph it at slow shutter speeds, underexposing one-half to one stop to saturate the colors. Zoom in close to eliminate the subject, leaving only the reflection itself, perhaps including a dark rock off center or floating leaves in the image.

Look for bright, warm reflections in dark, cool water. Typically a reflection is about one stop darker than the subject. Thus, expose for the subject itself, which results in a darker reflection with well-saturated colors. If the reflection is more than one stop darker than the subject and you want to even out the light difference between the subject and reflection, use a graduated neutral-density filter.

Polarizing filters remove the glare from the water surface. In some cases this eliminates the reflections altogether, allowing you to shoot what is beneath the surface of a shallow tide pool or pond. In others, the polarizer saturates the colors of both the subject and its reflection. Experiment with the polarizer and your position to get the effect that you want.

TIP
Use shutter speeds of 1/4 second to 1 second to create silky smooth waterfalls and running water.

Photograph the cascading water of waterfalls and rapids in two ways that can result in very different images of the same landscape. First, to achieve a silky smooth flow as in Plate 10, use a tripod and shutter speeds of 1/4 second to 1 second. Try a warming filter to counteract the bluish cast that may reflect from the water. Alternatively, to record the power of a raging torrent, use a fast shutter speed to stop the water's motion. In either case, try a polarizer to eliminate unwanted glare from both the water's surface and any surrounding areas wet from spray. Also, look for rainbows often accompanying waterfalls.

CLOSE-UP AND MACRO PHOTOGRAPHY

Close-up and macro photography allow you to record the smallest details and tiny slices of the surrounding environment. Inside this Lilliputian world there are myriad hidden compositions on lichen-covered rocks, weathered tree trunks, the ground at your feet, and just about anywhere else you can imagine. These compositions include individual shots of small subjects such as insects, as in Plate 30, pictures within pictures such as a small cluster of wildflowers in an alpine meadow, as in Plate 31, and more complex macroscapes filled with patterns, textures, and colors—like landscapes, only smaller—such as the tundra flowers in Plate 32. All you need to shoot these is a bit of patience, some extra gear, and an eye for the not-so-obvious.

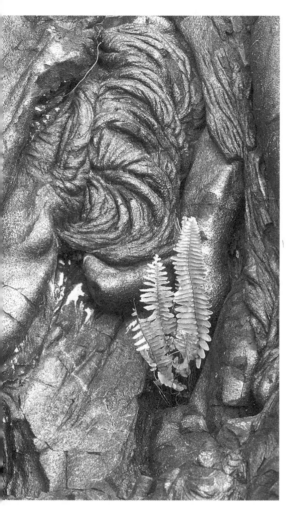

Figure 5-11 Lava Formation,
Volcanoes National Park, Hawaii

Gear

To photograph small scenes and subjects requires that you have enough magnification to fill the frame with them at close range. Standard lenses usually do not have enough without help from accessories. True *macro lenses* can be used like any other lens, but also provide the magnification and close focusing needed to photograph even the smallest bugs and flower parts. A macro lens can replace a normal lens, and excellent "macro zooms" are now available with a close-up capability that approaches that of true macro lenses.

Most lenses provide a magnification of $^1/_{10}$ or 1:10. That is, the subject can only be as big as one-tenth of life-size in the slide or negative. This means that you can fill a 35mm frame with a subject that is about 10 inches by 15 inches or bigger. To photograph small scenes, such as a cluster of flowers, you need a magnification of between 1:10 and 1:4, or one-tenth to one-fourth life-size. Individual flowers, bugs, and other small subjects, like the insect in Plate 30, require magnification of about 1:4 to 1:1, or one-fourth life-size to life-size. For example, at a magnification of 1x or 1:1, you can fill the frame with something as small as a nickel. Really small subjects, such as a feeding mosquito, require magnifications greater than 1:1, for which you need specialized gear as well as more time and patience than most of us can afford. Magnifications in the range of 1:4 to 1:2, which are sufficient for most close-up photography, can be easily obtained without buying a true macro lens.

Any lens can provide this level of magnification by adding any one of several relatively inexpensive accessories. Extension tubes, which fit between your camera and lens, allow any focal-length lens to focus closer. These glassless tubes come in a variety of widths and can be stacked together to adjust the amount of extension needed to get the shot you want. With greater extension, the magnification increases. Macro teleconverters are also now available with variable-length extension built in. These provide a complete range of magnification in one accessory.

Both of these work well with fixed-length lenses but can be tricky to use with zoom lenses. However, close-up lenses or diopters can be easily used with both types. These lightweight accessories look like a thick filter and screw onto the front of your lens just like any other filter. They are available in a variety of magnifications and can be stacked to increase power. Use only the higher-quality, more expensive models; cheap ones save a few dollars but can noticeably degrade image quality, especially at the edges. Diopters are usually available in one or two filter sizes, which means you may have to use a step-up ring to fit them to your particular lens.

Focusing

One of the biggest challenges in close-up photography is producing an image in which the subject is completely in focus. The closer you get to your subject, the more narrow the depth of field and thus the harder it is to have your subject completely in focus. However, several tricks help overcome this problem and produce more satisfying pictures.

First, use a tripod or other camera support. It is very difficult, if not impossible, to hold a camera steady enough to get sharp images when depth of field is very narrow. When shooting at ground level, your support should put the camera as close to the ground as possible.

> **TIP**
>
> For close-up shots, use an aperture of f/16 or smaller, focus on the subject's front or most important parts, and make sure the camera back is parallel to the plane of the subject.

This is difficult, if not impossible, with most tripods unless the legs of the tripod can open completely. To get even lower, use a clamp with a small ball head attached to a tripod leg or other ground-level support. When working at ground level, use a closed-cell foam pad to keep your knees clean and comfortable.

Second, maximize depth of field by using the smallest aperture possible, at least f/16. Third, keep the film plane, i.e., the back of the camera, as parallel as possible to the subject. Once you have set up your shot, step to one side of the camera and see if the subject and back of the camera are parallel. Finally, minimize subject movement. For example, when shooting flowers in a meadow, use your jacket, a ground sheet, or a pack to block the wind. Flash can also be used to freeze motion.

When you cannot get the subject entirely in focus, then focus on the most important part of the subject such as its eyes, as in Plate 30, or the front of the subject and let the rest of the image recede into a blurred background. For example, when photographing wildflowers make sure that the nearest petals or flowers are in focus, with ones further away out of focus. You can also create unique images by focusing on one element, such as one flower among flowers of a different color or a tiny spider on one flower, then purposely limiting the depth of field. The one focused element will dramatically stand out from an often mysteriously blurred background.

Even, diffused light like that found in shadows or overcast days is best for close-up shots. However, you can still take satisfying images in the bright, contrasty light of midday by shooting in the shadows or by controlling the light that is falling on or behind your subject. Eliminate harsh direct light by casting a shadow with a jacket, a companion, or even yourself, or by diffusing the light with a thin, white shirt or a collapsible diffuser. Alternatively, you can create more even lighting by filling in the subject's shadowy areas with flash or a reflector such as a space blanket, pot lid, or collapsible commercial model.

To better isolate and emphasize your subject, look for a darker, contrasting background. If you cannot find one, create one by casting a shadow behind the subject with a pack or jacket. Or position the pack or jacket—or anything else made from a nonreflective fabric in a dark, contrasting color—well behind the subject. Then adjust your depth of field so that the item provides an unrecognizably blurred background.

Always use your depth-of-field preview button to see what is really going in your photograph before you actually take it. Make sure the right parts of the subject are in focus and look for any distracting, out-of-focus highlights in the background. Unfortunately, the viewfinder will become very dim when shooting at the small apertures often used in close-up photography, making it more difficult to see what is in focus. When this happens, cup your hands around the eyepiece to block outside light and wait until your pupils dilate. After a brief period, you will be better able to see.

PHOTOGRAPHING WILDLIFE

Wildlife is often an exciting part of backcountry or exotic adventure. To maximize your chances of getting great shots, research the animals and area that you plan to be in before leaving home. Public libraries are full of books and magazines that can help you learn about an animal's preferred habitat types, behaviors that may make it easier to photograph—such as elk when they are rutting or sage grouse lekking—and other information that will make wildlife easier to capture on film.

Information on the animals and lands under their stewardship is also available from a variety of government agencies at the federal, state or provincial, and local levels that manage parks, refuges, and resources. Contact the administrative offices nearest you or in the area where you plan to be to find out how to get any available publications that may be helpful. Also, talk with rangers and biologists, who are often more than happy to share their knowledge with you. The more you learn about the animal that you want to photograph and its habitat, the greater your chances of taking successful phototgraphs.

Wildlife portraits are most easily taken in the many zoos, game farms, and game parks where animals are more habituated to people. Check to see if there are any in the vicinity where you will be traveling. Such places offer relatively easy access to animals that might otherwise be impossible to photograph in the wild. However, shots of listless animals behind bars will not be very pleasing; also be careful of the background, avoiding obvious human-made distractions and unnatural surroundings.

Approaching Animals

In the field, once you have found the wildlife you want to photograph, wait and watch before approaching. Observing their movements and behavior can help you best position yourself and anticipate the best shot. Consider photographing before you approach, when the animal is a relatively small part of the image and the surrounding environment is equally important. Some of the best wildlife shots show animals as a part of their habitat.

Before approaching, evaluate the best direction of approach. Consider the direction of light and backdrop that will produce the most effective image as well as the terrain itself, especially looking for any hazards. Approach wildlife slowly and casually, avoiding direct eye contact, quick movements, or any other behavior that might be considered threatening. Do not try to sneak up on them or surprise them. Rather, let them see you and get accustomed to your presence. If you approach too quickly or closely, animals become agitated and may flee. At that point, back off a bit and wait before approaching again. Eventually you will learn how close you can get and work yourself into the best position.

A few words of caution: never get too close or corner a wild animal. Even a seemingly benign backyard squirrel can inflict serious injury. Be sure to leave an escape route for both yourself and the animal. More importantly, be careful around animals with eggs or young. Jumpy mothers may abandon or defend their young. If you are photographing an animal as it moves to a feeding area or a nest, watch how the animal comes and goes. Then position yourself so that you do not block that route.

Concealing yourself near a nest, den, watering hole, game trail, or feeding area can result in excellent images. Cars make excellent blinds, especially in parks. When shooting from your car, use a window clamp or beanbag to support the camera. A variety of blinds are commercially available or can be made from camouflage materials. However, tents, thick vegetation, dark shadows, or just about anything else that conceals your form and hides your movements also works quite well. A blind may not be enough for the most wary animals. You may also have to cover your scent with one of the many animal scents available through hunting stores.

Techniques

An animal's eyes add life to the picture and are usually the first thing that people notice in a photograph of an animal. As long as the eye is sharply in focus, then the photograph can be successful even if the parts of the animal farthest away are less sharp. So when photographing an individual animal, focus on its eye, as in Plate 33, and with a group of animals, focus on the eye of the most prominent or closest individual. This is especially important when shooting with telephoto lenses over longer distances where the depth of field is often smaller than the animal.

The best types of light for wildlife photography are the diffuse light of a bright but overcast day, or the warm sidelight of early morning and late afternoon. Such light brings out the detail in animals' faces and accentuates their color. Avoid

TIP

When photographing wildlife, focus on the eyes, or just in front of the eyes.

the top light of a harsh midday sun, which casts shadows across animals' faces and creates too much contrast for appealing photographs.

Adding a touch of flash can greatly enhance animal portraits, even at longer distances when using telephoto lenses. Try fill flash to open up facial shadows, add a sparkle to the eyes, and add warmth to the photograph. Flash can also be an effective way to stop the action of smaller, quicker animals such as songbirds. But be careful not to startle the animal or black out the background. If your flash allows, reduce the output from the flash by one and a half stops when taking daylight pictures, to create a more natural-looking image. Using flash with animals can result in red eye, especially if it is relatively dark and the flash becomes the primary light source. To avoid this, move the flash a foot or two to the side of the camera, aiming it at the animal, before taking the picture.

To freeze the motion of a walking animal, shoot at 1/125 second or 1/250 second. For a flying or running animal, shoot at 1/500 second. (See Table 1-1, chapter 1, for guidelines.) You can use much slower shutter speeds by tracking the animal with your camera mounted on a tripod, waiting for it to stop moving before shooting. You can even get it to stop by snapping your fingers or making clicking or kissing sounds as it is moving around. When it stops to identify the source of the noise, take the picture.

When the light is too low to use stop-action shutter speeds of at least 1/125 second or faster, it is difficult to get sharp portraits of moving animals. Slightly fuzzy animal shots are very distracting to the viewer. So slow the shutter down to capture blurred impressions of animals, which can be a very effective way to show speed and motion, as discussed in chapter 1. Try using automatic fill flash or rear-curtain synch flash, if your camera has such features, with slow shutter speeds to create very interesting effects such as a running deer followed by the blur of its motion.

TIP

When photographing animals, position them so that they are moving into or looking into the frame.

Animal photographs that show humanlike expressions or behaviors, especially humorous ones, are often the most effective. For example, the mother bear's look of concern adds impact to the photograph in Plate 11. Pictures of a fierce grizzly bear scratching itself with a look of sheer bliss on its face, a lion licking its chops before dining, or a mother marmot and her baby touching noses as if kissing will always captivate your viewer. Before pressing the shutter release button, watch the animal, looking for behaviors or actions that will at least produce interesting pictures and at best ones with fun expressions.

Avoid placing the animal in the center of the image. Rather, position it at one of the "rule of thirds" intersection points, as discussed in chapter 1. In frame-filling portraits, position the animal's eye at one of the upper intersection points. Try to have the animal looking into the frame or at the viewer; an animal gazing out of the frame will lead your viewer right out of the photograph. Or have the animal turning and looking back at you. The same is true for moving animals; try to shoot them moving into the frame rather than out of it. Finally, look for simple, contrasting backgrounds that will accentuate the animal. Watch for background distractions, especially when using telephoto lenses that compress the scene and make branches behind the animal look like they are going in one ear and out the other.

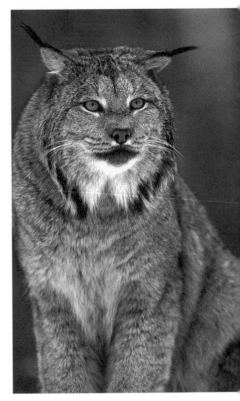

Gear

You do not have to have an extremely long telephoto lens to get good wildlife shots. A 200mm to 300mm lens is ideal for including wildlife as part of a scene, such as the whale in Plate 9, as well as full-body shots of bigger animals such as the bears in Plate 11. With patience and the right position, you can even get smaller and more skittish animals. However, a 400mm or

Figure 5-12 Canadian Lynx. Montana

longer lens may be required for smaller animals, frame-filling portraits of bigger ones, and full-body shots of animals that are difficult to approach, as in Figure 5-12. Such lenses are expensive, but they can often be rented from camera shops.

Two accessories expand the range of animals that you can shoot with a telephoto lens. Focal length can be extended with a teleconverter, which is available in 1.4x and 2x configurations. While these may extend the reach of your telephoto, their use results in a loss of light and quality. Using a 1.4x teleconverter results in a one-stop loss of light and a small, but usually acceptable, reduction in image quality. On the other hand, using a 2x converter results in a two-stop light loss and a generally unacceptable quality reduction. Because of this light loss, you may not be able to use teleconverters in low-light situations. Their use is limited to relatively fast lenses with maximum apertures of f/4 or bigger, although a 1.4x may work acceptably with a good-quality 400mm f/5.6 lens. Stick with the converters designed for your lens. Use of other teleconverters can result in poor quality and vignetting, which means that the corners of your photograph will be noticeably darker than the rest of the image.

While teleconverters extend the reach of telephotos, extension tubes bring it in closer to the camera. Most telephotos will not focus closely enough to make full-frame shots of small subjects such as sparrows, butterflies, or field mice. But adding extension tubes between the camera and lens decreases the minimum focusing distance and allows you to shoot such small subjects. However, use of extension tubes results in some light loss (but no reduction in image quality), making them difficult to use with slower lenses and in low-light situations.

GLOSSARY

Aperture: The size of the opening in the lens through which light passes into the camera, usually measured in f-stops or f-numbers.

Aperture Priority Mode: An automatic exposure mode in which you select the lens aperture and the camera selects the appropriate shutter speed. Consult your camera's manual for how to use this mode with your camera.

Automatically balanced fill flash: Either a built-in flash or a separate unit mounted on your camera's hot shoe that communicates with the camera to get exposure settings and ambient light level as read by the camera's through-the-lens (TTL) light meter (referred to as TTL flash), and then calculates the appropriate flash output. When you take the picture, the flash reads the light reflecting back to the camera and shuts the flash off when the correct light level has been reached.

"B" or "Bulb" setting: Shutter speed setting that keeps the shutter open for as long as you hold down the shutter release button, either manually or with a cable extension.

Backlighting: When the light source is behind the subject and in the face of the photographer.

Bracketing: Taking a series of shots under and over the initial exposure you determined to be correct.

Center-weighted meter: A type of light meter that assigns more importance to the light in the center of the scene, usually outlined by a large circle in the middle of your viewfinder, than the light from the surrounding area.

Contrast: The range of tones, from the darkest to the lightest, in your photograph or the scene you are shooting. Low contrast is a narrow range; for example, everything in the scene is more or less the same tone. High contrast is a broad range; for example, a scene includes tones at both ends of the spectrum, from black to white.

Depth of field: The zone of acceptably sharp focus in front of and behind the subject or point at which the lens is focused. Everything in front of and behind this zone is out of focus.

Depth-of-field preview button: A camera feature that allows you to view the image through the aperture setting you have selected. When you look through your viewfinder, you see the image as it looks using the largest aperture. This lets in more light, making it easier to see and focus on what you are photographing, but does not show you the actual depth of field. Thus, your picture may not look like what you saw through the viewfinder. Depth-of-field preview allows you to see what your photograph will actually look like.

Depth-of-field scale: A scale marked on the barrel of some cameras that indicates the depth of field for the particular aperture at which the lens is set and the distance at which the lens is focused. Many modern autofocus and zoom lenses omit this scale.

Direct light: Light that travels from the sun or other light source directly to the subject or scene without being significantly impacted along the way.

Directional lighting: Light that comes predominantly from one direction.

Evaluative meter: A type of light meter that reads the central area in the viewfinder much like a center-weighted meter, but also divides the surrounding area into zones that are evaluated relative to each other and the central area. See *center-weighted meter*.

Exposure: The amount of light required to record the image you want on film, usually expressed in terms of an aperture and shutter speed combination at a given film speed, or Exposure Value (EV).

Exposure compensation: Light meters provide exposure settings, usually shutter speed and aperture combinations, that result in a medium-toned photograph. This means that darker items will appear too light or lighter items too dark. Exposure compensation means you let in more light than indicated by your meter when metering a light-toned subject, and you let in less light when metering dark objects.

Exposure guidelines: Exposure settings, expressed in terms of shutter speed and aperture, based on light conditions rather than light meter readings; for example, the Sunny f/16 Rule is a guideline for exposure under a bright sun.

Fill flash: Use of flash in conjunction with sunlight, the primary light source, to fill in any shadows or highlight the subject.

Film speed: The sensitivity of film to light. Low-speed films are less sensitive and require more light to record an image; high-speed films are more sensitive and require less light.

Filter: An accessory made of glass, plastic, or resin, which is placed in front of the lens to filter the light entering the lens, thus changing the character of the light that strikes the film.

Flare: Nonimage-forming light caused by scattering and reflecting of light inside the lens, which results in odd shapes and spots of light on a photograph.

Focal length: The distance between the optical center of the lens and the film when the lens is focused to infinity.

Focusing screen: The screen inside the camera's viewfinder on which the image is focused.

Frame: The boundaries of the rectangle defined by the camera's viewfinder, and thus the edges of the resulting photograph.

Front-lighting: When the light source is in front of the subject and behind the photographer.

f-stop: An indicator of aperture size, also expressed as f/stop, based on the ratio between the aperture and focal length of a lens. The larger the stop—the number after or under the "f"—the smaller the aperture. For example, f/22 is a very small aperture, while f/2 is a very large aperture.

Graduated neutral-density filter: Rectangular filter in which one half is clear and

Glossary

the other half is darker by one, two, or three stops, allowing you to balance bright highlights and dark shadows, or other situations in which the background is bright and the foreground darker.

Gray card: A card colored with the standard gray tone, called 18 percent gray, which represents the medium tone to which light meters are calibrated.

Haze filter: A filter that removes light in the blue to ultraviolet spectrum, thus eliminating or reducing atmospheric haze.

Hyperfocal distance: Focal length at which everything from halfway between the camera and that point out to infinity is in focus.

Indirect light: Light that has been deflected, scattered, or reflected so that it seems not to come from any one direction and therefore illuminates a subject very evenly.

ISO number: An indicator of film speed. The higher the number, the faster the film and the less light required to make a given photograph.

Lens-shutter camera: See *point-and-shoot camera.*

Light meter: Measures the amount of light traveling through the lens to the camera's viewfinder, which in an SLR is effectively the same as the amount of light striking the film once the reflex mirror flips up and the shutter opens.

Low light: Light levels that are dim enough to require the use of slow shutter speeds (less than 1/60 second), wide apertures, tripods, and/or fast film. These usually occur early in the morning, in the evening, inside thick forests, under heavily overcast skies, and indoors.

Macro lens: A lens that can be focused closely enough to photograph small subjects such as individual flowers and insects. A true macro lens can make near life-size or larger images on film, which means filling a 35mm frame with a subject the size of a small coin.

Magic hour: The best time to photograph on sunny days; lasts from about a half hour to an hour before and after both sunrise and sunset.

Matrix meter: Same as *Evaluative meter.*

Medium tone: A tone that is neither very light nor very dark, but midway between these extremes; for example, the medium gray, in a tonal range from black to white, of the standard *gray card.*

Metering: Measuring the amount of reflected light that is entering the camera's lens. To "meter on" an object means to measure the amount of light reflecting off that particular object.

Multiple exposures: Multiple images recorded on the same frame of film.

Natural light: Light from a natural source such as the sun, moon, or stars; in most photography, natural light comes primarily from the sun.

Normal lens: A lens for a 35mm camera with a focal length between 40mm and 60mm.

Opening up: Increasing the size of the lens's aperture, thus letting more light pass through the lens and increasing the depth of field; for example, opening up from f/22 to f/5.6.

Overexposure: When your subject or key objects in your photograph appear lighter than you wanted them to, which means that too much light reached the film.

Panning: Moving the camera to keep a moving subject in the viewfinder while shooting.

Point-and-shoot camera: A completely automatic camera with which you have limited control. The camera determines the speed of the film you load in, and then sets the aperture and shutter speed based on its meter reading. Also called a *lens-shutter camera.*

Polarizing filter: A filter that removes light waves not traveling straight through the lens (along a place perpendicular to the front of the lens), which reduces glare, reflections, and haze as well as saturating colors.

Print film: Film that produces a negative, from which prints are made, when processed.

Program Mode: An automatic exposure mode that selects both shutter speed and aperture. Consult your camera's manual for how to use this mode with your camera.

Reciprocity: The relationship between the variables of shutter speed and aperture, both of which are calibrated in stops, whereby an increase in one variable combined with a comparable decrease in the other results in the same exposure value.

Shutter Priority Mode: An automatic exposure mode in which you manually select the shutter speed and the camera selects the appropriate aperture.

Shutter release cable: A cable that attaches to the camera body and is used to release the shutter without pressing the shutter release button.

Shutter speed: The amount of time the shutter remains open, and thus the amount of time the film is exposed to the light coming through the lens.

Sidelighting: When light comes predominantly from one side of the subject.

Single-lens reflex: A camera that has a single lens and a reflex mirror inside which reflects the light coming in through the lens up to the viewfinder, allowing you to see what will actually be photographed. When you press the shutter release button, the mirror swings out of the way.

Skylight filter: A filter that eliminates light waves in the blue to ultraviolet spectrum and adds a very slight pinkish, or warm, cast to the image.

Slide film: Film that produces transparent images which must be illuminated from behind for viewing.

SLR: See *single-lens reflex.*

Spotlighting: Light that illuminates a subject with a single beam of light which emerges from a hole in cloud cover, forest canopy, structures, etc.

Spot metering: A type of light metering in which the meter only evaluates the light intensity in a small circle located in the center of the viewfinder.

Stop: A relative measure of the quantity of light in which any given value is twice as much light as the preceding value and half as much light as the next value. F-numbers, shutter speeds, and film speeds (ISO numbers) are all calibrated in stops. For example, an aperture of f/5.6 lets in twice as much light as f/8 but half as much as f/2.8; or a shutter speed of 1/250 second lets in twice as much light as 1/500 second and half as much as 1/125 second.

Stopping down: Decreasing the size of the lens's aperture, thus reducing the amount of light passing through the lens and increasing depth of field; for example, stopping down from f/5.6 to f/22.

Sunny f/16 Rule: The correct exposure, for any film, when photographing a front-lit subject on a sunny day is an aperture of f/16 and a shutter speed *nearest* to 1/ISO, where ISO is the speed of the film in your camera.

Teleconverter: An optical accessory placed between the camera's body and lens that increases the magnification by 1.4x to 2x.

Telephoto lens: A lens with a focal length longer than 70 mm.

Tone: The shade of a color, or how dark or light an object is.

Top-lighting: When light comes from above the subject.
TTL: Literally, through the lens, referring to the light that is actually coming through the lens to strike the film. TTL light metering measures the light coming through the lens to the film; TTL flashes use the through-the-lens light reading from the light meter to control flash output.
Ultraviolet (UV) filter: A filter that eliminates light waves in the ultraviolet spectrum, which you do not see but which the film records as a slight bluish cast.
Underexposure: When your subject or key objects in your photograph appear darker than you wanted them to, which means that not enough light reached the film.
Vignetting: A darkening at the corners of slides or prints, usually caused by using teleconverters or lens hoods that are not matched to the lens to which they are attached, as well as by stacking too many filters on the front of the lens.
Warming filter: A filter that adds a slight yellow-amber cast to an image.
Wide-angle lens: A lens with a focal length less than 40mm.
Zoom lens: A lens with a range of focal lengths.

BIBLIOGRAPHY

For an in-depth discussion of Art Wolfe's approach to nature photography, see *The Art of Photographing Nature* by Martha Hill and Art Wolfe (New York: Crown Publishers, 1993).

Eastman Kodak. *The Joy of Photography.* New York: Addison-Wesley, 1979.
———. *More Joy of Photography.* New York: Addison-Wesley, 1988.
Lepp, George. *Beyond the Basics: Innovative Techniques for Nature Photography.* Los Osos, Calif.: Lepp & Associates, 1993.
Levey, Marc. *The 35mm Film Source Book.* Boston: Focal Press, 1992.
McDonald, Joe. *The Wildlife Photographer's Field Manual.* Amherst, N.Y.: Amherst Media, 1992.
Patterson, Freeman. *Photography of Natural Things.* Toronto: Van Nostrand Reinhold, 1982.
Peterson, Bryan F. *Learning to See Creatively.* New York: Amphoto, 1988.
———. *People in Focus.* New York: Amphoto, 1993.
Rowell, Galen. *Mountain Light.* San Francisco: Sierra Club Books, 1986.
———. *The Art of Adventure.* San Francisco: Collins Publishers, 1989.
Shaw, John. *The Nature Photographer's Complete Guide to Professional Field Techniques.* New York: Amphoto, 1984.
———. *Closeups in Nature.* New York: Amphoto, 1987.

INDEX

Index

ABOUT THE AUTHORS

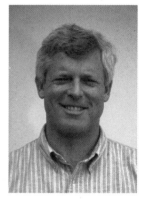

Mark Gardner has been actively pursuing outdoor adventures with his camera in hand for over twenty-five years. An avid climber, backpacker, mountain biker, skier, sea kayaker, and river rafter, he has taught photography on field trips organized by The Mountaineers. He lives in Bellevue, Washington.

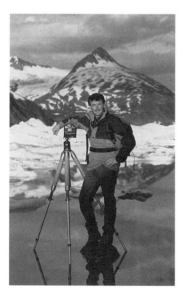

Art Wolfe is one of the most celebrated wildlife/nature photographers in the United States. His work is published regularly in such periodicals as *Audubon, Islands, Life, National Geographic, National Wildlife, Outside,* and *Smithsonian* and has been the subject of numerous books, including *Light on the Land; Bears: Their Life and Behavior; Penguins, Puffins, and Auks; The Art of Photographing Nature* (co-authored with Martha Hill), and *Migrations.* He is a member of the Advisory Board of the Wildlife Conservation Society and lives in Seattle.

THE MOUNTAINEERS, founded in 1906, is a nonprofit outdoor activity and conservation club, whose mission is "to explore, study, preserve, and enjoy the natural beauty of the outdoors. . . ." Based in Seattle, Washington, the club is now the third-largest such organization in the United States, with 15,000 members and five branches throughout Washington State.

The Mountaineers sponsors both classes and year-round outdoor activities in the Pacific Northwest, which include hiking, mountain climbing, ski-touring, snowshoeing, bicycling, camping, kayaking and canoeing, nature study, sailing, and adventure travel. The club's conservation division supports environmental causes through educational activities, sponsoring legislation, and presenting informational programs. All club activities are led by skilled, experienced volunteers, who are dedicated to promoting safe and responsible enjoyment and preservation of the outdoors.

The Mountaineers Books, an active, nonprofit publishing program of the club, produces guidebooks, instructional texts, historical works, natural history guides, and works on environmental conservation. All books produced by The Mountaineers are aimed at fulfilling the club's mission.

If you would like to participate in these organized outdoor activities or the club's programs, consider a membership in The Mountaineers. For information and an application, write or call The Mountaineers, Club Headquarters, 300 Third Avenue West, Seattle, Washington 98119; (206) 284-6310.

Send or call for our catalog of more than 300 outdoor titles:

The Mountaineers Books
1001 SW Klickitat Way, Suite 201
Seattle, WA 98134
1-800-553-4453 / e-mail:mbooks@mountaineers.org